Nowadays, we are all familiar with the concept of the aura, which is, in fact, a subtle body of energy that is found around and inside the human body. An ever-increasing number of healers, scientists, and physicians have discovered that by treating the aura, it is possible to exert a positive influence on mind, body, and spirit.

Reiki is a method that is rapidly gaining in popularity; it is based on the creation of a link between cosmic energy and an individual's personal energy in order to improve his or her condition.

Years of study and treatments prompted Bill Waites to create a practical method for treating and healing the human aura by means of Reiki. This method is called "Aura-Reiki," and is described in this practical guide.

Aura-Reiki is an effective and simple method that enables the individual to enjoy a good quality of life, longevity, and maximal health. It can be self-administered, or administered in a small group.

Bill Waites, a former lawyer and economist, gave up a flourishing legal practice and business in order to study Reiki at its source in the Far East: Japan, China, and India. Master Naharo, a well-known guru and Reiki Master from Poona, India, was Waites' first teacher.

ASTROLOG - THE HEALING SERIES

Holistic Healing
Rachel Lewin

Feng Shui
Richard Taylor and Wang Tann

Reiki
Bill Waites and Master Naharo

Bach Flower Remedies
David Lord

Aromatherapy
Marion Wayman

Reflexology
Nathan B. Strauss

Shiatsu
Nathan B. Strauss

Feng Shui for the Modern City
Richard Taylor

Shiatsu for Lovers
Nathan B. Strauss

Color Healing: A Practical Guide
Graham Travis

Aura-Reiki
Bill Waites

Fifty Massage Points for Self-Healing
Nathan B. Strauss

Bill Waites

Aura-Reiki

A Practical Guide for Using Reiki to Heal the Aura

Astrolog Publishing House

Astrolog Publishing House
P. O. Box 1123, Hod Hasharon 45111, Israel
Tel: 972-9-7412044
Fax: 972-9-7442714
E-Mail: info@astrolog.co.il
Astrolog Web Site: www.astrolog.co.il

© Bill Waites 2001

ISBN 965-494-107-4

Published by Astrolog Publishing House 2001

Printed in Israel
1 3 5 7 9 10 8 6 4 2

CONTENTS

Introduction

This book is intended for the educated reader who wants to utilize the profound knowledge embedded in alternative therapies for his own growth. The author of this book, Bill Waites, who has studied and researched various types of healing, has developed and refined a unique system of healing called "Aura-Reiki". This system is presented here clearly and in full detail.

The first part of the book presents the theoretical premises in great detail. Upon reading this section, you will understand the essence of the aura and the primary "entry gates" of the aura — the chakras.

Once you have grasped the theoretical background, we move on to the practical part which is amazingly simple. The first stage is the diagnosis which consists of seven steps — each step corresponds to the chakras, from the first to the seventh. The chakras are the surest and most simple way of reaching the aura and its various layers, of treating blockages and excess energy or energy depletion in the aura.

After reading the section regarding the first chakra, you evaluate the state of your first chakra (with time and experience, you will also be able to do this for others and to treat them). This evaluation is done by answering questions such as: Is this chakra balanced? Am I lacking energy in this chakra? Do I have too much energy in this chakra?

You then rate your answers on a scale of one to nine, where five reresents a balanced state. One to four shows a chakra with too little energy — one means a total lack of energy (which is the most common state) — and six to nine shows a chakra with too much energy (with nine representing an overflow of energy).

Once you have rated the energy level of your first

chakra, you then move on to the second chakra and repeat the process there until you have covered all seven chakras. At this stage, you will have seven different scores (one for each chakra). It is important that all the chakras are rated in the same time frame — the evaluations of all the chakras should be done in one sitting — as the energetic states of the chakras fluctuate. Now put the chakras in order from the one with the least amount of energy to the one with the most amount of energy. If there are two or more chakras with the same rating, they are grouped together.

For example:

The scores:
First chakra: 1 2 **3** 4 5 6 7 8 9
Second chakra: 1 2 3 **4** 5 6 7 8 9
Third chakra: 1 2 3 4 5 6 **7** 8 9
Fourth chakra: 1 **2** 3 4 5 6 7 8 9
Fifth chakra: 1 2 3 4 5 6 7 **8** 9
Sixth chakra: 1 2 3 4 **5** 6 7 8 9
Seventh chakra: 1 2 3 4 5 6 **7** 8 9
(The underlined digit is the score for that chakra.)

The order:
1 — fourth chakra
2 — first chakra
3 — second chakra
4 — sixth chakra
5 — third and seventh chakras
6 — fifth chakra

The fourth chakra has a very obvious lack of energy, while the fifth chakra has too much energy. Both of these chakras which received extreme ratings, will be treated by Reiki in order to bring them back into balance.

Treating the aura with Reiki is very simple and is done through the chakras — and this is where the simplicity and genius of the Aura-Reiki system lies. All we need to do is treat the two (or more) chakras that received extreme scores. The Reiki enables us to reach the essence of the problem directly, when treating both ourselves and others.

The therapeutic part of the Aura-Reiki system in this book is short and gives an explanation about Reiki, its principles (Reiki can only be used once its principles have been studied and internalized), and the seven hand positions — one for each chakra. All you need to do is lay your hands in the position that is suited to the chakra that you are treating, and to mentally focus and ask the higher universal power to balance the chakra (this request can be phrased however you wish). Treatment starts with the chakra or chakras that are lacking energy (in the extreme) and then moves on to the chakra or chakras that have too much energy (again in the extreme). [Reiki can be used to treat others according to the same principles. The only thing done differently is the position of the hands. In the practical part of this book we demonstrate the different hand positions for self-treatment and when treating others. More information can be found in the book *The Complete Reiki Course* by Master Naharo with Gail Radford, published by Astrolog Publishing House, ISBN 965-494-119-8]

In order for the Aura-Reiki treatment to be successful, three consecutive days of laying of the hands is required. It is important to remember that the diagnosis and treatment of the states of the chakras are correct at that particular time. If you rate your chakras about two weeks after you first did it (without treatment), you will most probably find that there's a difference in the balances of the chakras. Having said that, the basic rule stays the same — we first identify the chakras with the least and the most energy, and then we use Reiki to balance them.

As you can see, the theoretical-diagnostic section is long and full of information, while the treatment section is short and succinct. This is because diagnosis is difficult and demands a lot of knowledge, while the Reiki treatment is easier to grasp. I am certain that with time and practice, you will know how to diagnose yourself and others quickly, so that each treatment won't take more than an hour.

We hope that this book contributes to your quest for better health.

The energetic system and the subtle bodies

Beyond what we can easily see and touch – material matter – is the electromagnetic field – the aura – and the subtle bodies, which are composed of thin, subtle, energetic matter. A well-known law of physics states that energy never disappears – it just changes form. As the physical body dies and continues the cycle of life through decomposition and composition, so our more subtle bodies do not disappear, but ostensibly change their form. This is the force that drives the person – body, mind, and spirit. When the spirit departs the body, the flesh, which was once active and creative, is left lifeless.

Our being is activated by a complex and complicated energetic system, without which the life and existence of the physical body would not be possible. This system includes the subtle energetic bodies, the chakras or the energy centers, and the meridians or the energy channels. In addition, a vast, indefinable universal force activates and directs our soul. The energetic bodies, chakras, and meridians function as valves which "reduce" the tremendous life force that we are incapable of receiving in all its power. We can only take it in small doses – each person according to his own capacity.

The aura

The aura is the electromagnetic field that surrounds the human body as well as every organism and object in the universe. When, for example, we see paintings of Christian saints with a circle of white or yellow light around their heads, or angels with their halos, we can see how people imagined the electromagnetic field looked. This is not just the imagination of the painters and artists, however, and these auras do not only surround saints or angels. The aura itself frequently resembles those in these paintings. It surrounds every creature, and every person, but the higher the person's energetic cleanliness and level of spiritual connection to the higher, divine energy levels, the higher the frequencies at which his electromagnetic field vibrates, creating the feeling of a "radiant" face, or "luminous" eyes. All of us, without exception, as well as the various animals, plants, and objects, are surrounded by electromagnetic fields of varying strength.

The electromagnetic field – the aura – has been known to people for many years. Through the ages, mystics, healers, shamans, clairvoyants, and people with supernatural powers have been able to feel and see the electromagnetic field around the human body. Many ancient sources, including the "Zohar" (the Book of Splendor) in the Jewish tradition and many ancient mystical works tell of the aura and relate to it in different ways. In general, however, there is an exceptional consensus among the ancient writers about the effect of external and internal influences on it, about what it symbolizes, and about its size and colors – even though the writers came from different places and encompassed most of the peoples of the world.

In the twentieth century, with the development of science,

more and more scientists began to take an interest in the mysteries of the electromagnetic field. Michael Farraday, Nikola Tesla, and Thomas Edison were among the many scientists who encountered the electromagnetic field surrounding the human body during their experiments, and were astounded at their discoveries. But it was only in the fourth decade of the twentieth century, a time when many scientists started performing pre-planned experiments in order to comprehend and discover the nature of the electromagnetic field, that the entire subject was given a significant push forward.

The best-known of these scientists is the Russian, S. D. Kirlian, who developed Kirlian photography, a technology which can record the electromagnetic field of living organisms.

Today, this method of documentation is called "electro-photography." Electro-photography uses a phenomenon called "aura emission." The aura is the result of electron emission. In electro-photography, millions of electrons are emitted and move toward a special part of the camera, which absorbs them, creating magnificent and beautifully colored pictures of the patterns of energy emission.

In Kirlian photography, the feet and hands of the subject are usually photographed. The feet and hands are briefly exposed to high-frequency rays on the surface of the photographic plate, and the result is documented on the plate or photographic paper. When the plate or paper is developed, a magnificent picture of the electromagnetic field surrounding the hands or feet is revealed; astonishingly, the tip of each finger or toe has its own unique electromagnetic field. Surprisingly, Kirlian photography reinforced many theories concerning reflexology and acupuncture. When a certain area on the foot or hand, especially at the tips of the digits, had a weak, blocked, or punctured aura, it turned out that there were problems with the meridian that was linked to this point or reflex area (it could be any organ in the body). The development of the use of Kirlian photography solved many mysteries connected to our electromagnetic field, and gave a significant boost to complementary medicine. The photographic "proof" that every object in the universe is surrounded by an electromagnetic field stunned many people. Others saw in it concrete corroboration of what they believed or even felt and saw.

The publication of these works, findings, and research gave rise to an increase in interest and the desire to understand the electromagnetic field that surrounds the human being, and its effects on his sensations. Concurrently, the ability to understand the action of the electromagnetic field increased, as did the ways to positively influence its condition.

The electromagnetic field that surrounds every object can be positive or negative, perfect or deficient. But it is not static and immutable, or unaffected by external and internal factors. It is extremely dynamic and operates interactively with various internal and external factors. The organisms in the universe live in a perpetual state of energetic "give and take" among the various energetic fields, and they have to safeguard their electromagnetic fields against harm by negative or "energy-draining" electromagnetic fields. A great deal of research has shown that plants, for instance, shrink when there is negative or hostile energy in the vicinity of their electromagnetic field. Human beings are liable to feel the same way when they are in the presence of non-positive energy that emanates from various places, people, or objects. Occasionally, this sensitivity is translated into a "gut feeling" that causes us to move away from a certain place or person, or, conversely, to be attracted toward certain places, situations, or people.

Incompatibility between the electromagnetic fields of various people, or between a person and surroundings of some kind sometimes causes a feeling of inexplicable discomfort.

Sometimes, we find ourselves desperate to get away from certain people or places because of the lack of equilibrium that appears in their electromagnetic fields, because of an energetic incompatibility, or because one of the auras is too strong and dominant, emits non-positive frequencies, and so on. Although this feeling often does not have a conscious explanation, the information about the electromagnetic field of a certain person, environment, or object is picked up by our electromagnetic field. These messages pass through the electromagnetic field to the nervous system and affect the person's general feeling. Sometimes, they appear as signs that warn us to get away from the particular environment or person whose energy is not in harmony with ours, or is liable to harm our energetic equilibrium in some way. These signs will probably be expressed as a feeling of discomfort, agitation, rejection, anxiety, and so on.

Animals are extremely sensitive to electromagnetic fields. While their natural sensitivity does not exceed ours (although it does not always operate according to the same mechanisms), they react directly to the feeling of energy and to the messages they pick up. It is absolutely true that dogs and cats can sense energy that is non-positive or unsuitable for them in their surroundings, or sense the energetic type of person near them. The biochemical explanations for these feelings in animals are correct. However, they constitute merely a part of the feelings to which animals react (that is, they explain the phenomenon on the biochemical level, which is an addition to the energetic layer, and not a substitute for it), and only explain the phenomenon partially.

Every person, without exception, has the ability to sense electromagnetic fields, as well as see different levels of these fields, if he is conscious of this possibility and perseveres in developing it. The reason why most people do not see or feel them is that these senses, similar to the more physical senses (smell, hearing, etc.), are not sufficiently developed, and are even perhaps atrophied. The inability of many people to conceive of seeing something that they have never seen in a physical manner also has an inhibiting effect – to the point that the disbelief in the existence of the electromagnetic field is liable to affect their ability to see it.

Clairvoyants are able to discern the aura, and so are people who have honed their extrasensory visual powers. By observing the aura, it is possible to see that it contains different colors. Some of the colors are relatively "fixed." Others are changeable. The sum total of the colors may fade or intensify according to the person's mood and emotional, mental, and physical states. Of course, the person's spiritual state also has an enormous effect on the colors and size of the aura.

The main part of the color and energy in the aura is provided and activated by the action of the chakras.

In general, the aura spreads over a distance of 10-15cm from the physical body, and includes a number of energetic layers that are called the energetic bodies ("the subtle bodies").

The layers of the body – the energetic bodies

The layers of the body are other subtle bodies that exist around the physical body. Each one of these bodies, of which there are claimed to be four, five, six or even seven, has its own unique frequency. The ethereal body – the one that is closest to the physical body – has the lowest frequency. The astral and mental bodies have higher frequencies, while the spiritual body, and the bodies that are even higher than that have the highest frequencies.

It is very common for a person to sense somebody standing behind him, or beside him, without touching him – he feels a kind of touch, despite the physical distance. This is because the energetic bodies, all of which have their own "auras," are situated at different distances from the body, and are spread over broader areas than the physical body. Consequently, they may come into contact with the electromagnetic field of another person. The frequencies of the energetic bodies, their magnetic and electric current, dictate the person's electromagnetic field (aura) at different levels. Each one of the bodies has its own auric layer, and altogether, they constitute the electromagnetic field that contains all the information about us – our past, present, and future.

The bodies of the aura are in a perpetually interrelated system, and affect one another as well as the person's feelings, emotions, thinking, behavior, and health. As a result, a state of imbalance in one of the bodies leads to a state of imbalance in the others. Similarly, the development of the person's spirit and awareness affects the frequencies of each of the energetic bodies. When the frequencies of the bodies rise, this has an effect on the person's entire being – he becomes more energetic and vital, and is able to pick up and absorb higher energy frequencies, which affect the development of his spirit and awareness. This is how the perpetual interaction between the person's awareness and the state of his energetic bodies operates.

The physical body

The physical body is the first body. It is the "thickest" of all the bodies, tangible and material, visible and palpable. Our physical body works on the given physical levels, and is largely subject to the known physical laws. It comprises matter – atoms, cells, tissues, and organs. It is activated and controlled by various biochemical processes, and requires physical nourishment, motion, and evacuation. Perpetual destructive and regenerative processes occur simultaneously in it. When the person is young and his body is growing, the anabolic (building) forces operate more strongly than the catabolic (destructive) forces. This gradually changes as the body ages.

However, in spite of all this, if we look at things in depth, the physical body is far from being "physical," material, and absolutely stable. Our bodies, like the other objects in existence, are made up of atoms. Atoms are not stable and motionless – on the contrary. Atoms are in a state of perpetual motion, it is their density that creates the state of matter: solid, liquid, or gas. An astounding finding of quantum physics research revealed that the atom itself is changeable! Sometimes it behaves as a particle, and sometimes as a wave. The meaning of this incredible finding is that atoms are not just physical and stable, but also energetic. This means that we live in two worlds simultaneously.

The ethereal body

The ethereal body is the second body, and the first conscious body. It is also called the aura of the body. It is reminiscent of the physical body in shape, which is why it is sometimes called "the ethereal twin" or "the inner physical body."

The ethereal body carries inside it the forces that shape the physical body, the life energy that creates motion, and all the physical senses. The physical human body is nourished, develops, and exists through this more subtle energy field, and diseases begin their path to physical manifestation in it. For this reason, by treating the ethereal body, it is possible to treat physical conditions, since the ethereal body is a subtle bio-field that penetrates all matter. This subtle body is responsible for the person's general health and diverse activities. It carries within it the meridians, and they convey life energies and charge the body with energy.

Although the ethereal body is indiscernible to normal observation (with a little effort, however, it is possible to develop the ability to see it), it is composed of a material that belongs to the physical world, but it is invisible because it vibrates at a higher level than matter does. Frequently, we absorb and grasp it unconsciously. It is described as a misty material that surrounds the body at a distance of 2.5-10cm.

The ethereal body channels emotions (that affect and are affected by the emotional body), thoughts and intuitions (that are linked to the mental body) and spiritual information. Ultimately, the sum total is expressed in the material world.

The ethereal body is recreated in every incarnation, and dissipates a few days after the death of the physical body. It draws its energy from the sun via the solar plexus chakra and from the earth via the base chakra. It stores these energies and nourishes the physical body with them through the chakras and the meridians. These two forms of energy – sun energy and earth energy – ensure a living and breathing balance in the body's cells. When the body's need for energy is satisfied, the ethereal body liberates excess energy via the chakras and the pores in the skin, and it moves to a distance of 2.5-10cm from the physical body. In this way, an ethereal aura is created around the body. As we said before, this aura is the easiest one to see when we practice seeing the aura, and it is generally the first one we succeed in seeing. The rays of energy that leave the body envelop it in a protective layer. This layer protects the body against bacteria and viruses that are disease carriers, as well as against harmful substances, and safeguards its health. At the same time, it radiates life energy to the environment.

When we examine the protective quality that the ethereal layer creates, it is easy to understand that when the ethereal body is in optimal condition – or even slightly less – there is little chance that the person will succumb to a disease from the outside. In a case like this, the reason for the disease, if there is one, will stem from inside. These reasons can include negative thoughts, non-positive emotions, an unharmonious and stressful lifestyle, an unhealthy way of life, not paying heed to and not fulfilling the body's needs properly, and, of course, ingesting harmful substances such as nicotine, alcohol, and so on. All of the above use the strength of the ethereal body and exploit its energy stores, so that the body's protective sheath weakens, and gradually the window to "catching" external diseases opens. This is how "weak" areas and "holes" are formed in the aura. The flow of energy leaving the body so as to create an energetic sheath around it looks "distorted" instead of straight, or "confused" and unharmonious. This is how hollows, holes, or – in contrast – centers in which a great deal of energy accumulates and gets stuck are created in the human aura. This state enables negative energy and various external diseases, viruses, and bacteria to penetrate the person's physical body.

The problem does not end there, however. In addition, essential energy is liable to "leak" through the holes or gaps in the energetic sheath. This is how it is possible to identify states of disease by observing or feeling the ethereal body even before they manifest themselves in the physical body itself. Moreover, it is possible to treat them while they still exist only in the ethereal body by administering treatment to this body.

The ethereal body constitutes a body that connects the high energetic bodies to the physical body. It transmits information that is obtained through our physical senses to the mental and astral bodies, and simultaneously transmits energy and information from the superior bodies to the physical body. When the energy of the ethereal body is weakened, this communication may be harmed, and the person may feel indifferent and unconcerned mentally and emotionally.

The ethereal body, and similarly the physical body, reacts well to thoughts that are transmitted via the mental (conceptual) body. For this reason, work with mantras or positive affirmations has such a powerful effect on the health of the body.

Kirlian photography revealed that plants, especially trees and flowers, radiate a very similar energy to that radiated by the ethereal body. This is apparently one of the reasons that plants help us replenish our energy supply so powerfully, in different ways and forms. This energy can be found in aromatic oils, Bach flowers, and various medicinal herbs. When the person is outdoors, the plant kingdom pours this beneficial energy onto him, and it strengthens and renews his powers.

The astral (emotional) body

The astral body is the second energetic body, and it is also called the emotional body. This body carries within it all of our emotions, as well as the characteristics of our nature. It is directly affected by emotions, and it affects them. When the person is not particularly mature emotionally and spiritually, it is possible to make this body out as a kind of untidy cloud that moves in different directions. The more mature the person is in his emotions, thoughts, and character traits, the clearer and more defined the shape of his astral body will appear.

The astral body's aura is oval, and surrounds the body at a distance of 30-40cm. Every emotional change, every state of emotional imbalance, is projected to the entire aura via the astral body. This process is performed mainly by the chakras, and to a small extent by the pores in the skin. Outwardly, the person's emotional state is projected to the environment, and it is easy to discern, using our senses, when the person is angry, depressed, agitated, or upset, even if he seems indifferent. Sensitive people have no difficulty feeling the environmental effect of emotional projection when it is not balanced, and some of them feel disturbed and uncomfortable when they are in the vicinity of a person projecting non-positive emotions. Extremely sensitive people are liable to feel like this when a person is calm and relaxed, but at the same time carries various residual non-positive emotions from different times and events.

The astral aura is in perpetual motion. Because a person's basic character traits are expressed in the aura via basic colors, the astral aura is likely to change according to the person's emotions and emotional state.

For this reason, the colors of the astral body are perpetually changing. Negative emotions such as anger, depression, fear, and worry are expressed in dark colors and patches on the surface of the aura. In contrast, when the person feels love, happiness, joy, confidence in the universe, and courage, bright, variegated, "clean," shining colors can be discerned on his aura.

Of all the auras, one can say that the astral aura is the one that most powerfully shapes the average person's world-view and the reality in which he lives.

The astral body contains all the unresolved emotional conflicts, all the repressed emotions, the conscious and unconscious fears, the fears and emotions of rejection, the feelings of loneliness, aggressiveness, and lack of self-confidence. This emotional mass transmits its vibrations via the astral body to the world by sending unconscious messages to the universe.

This is extremely significant – these messages that we send to the world consciously or unconsciously via the astral body, are the ones that attract a certain reality to our lives. What we send is what we ultimately receive. Transmitting negative emotions brings negative events into our lives, thus fulfilling the (conscious or unconscious) pessimistic prophecies that invited these events in the first place. The energetic vibrations we transmit attract identical or similar energetic vibrations from the environment. Therefore, we repeatedly encounter situations, events, or people that constitute a mirror image of what we repress, fear, or want to get rid of.

However, this situation of a "mirror" meeting with people around us or with events that occur in our lives has a purpose. The unresolved emotions that are contained in our astral body are in a constant state of wanting to disappear. When we repeatedly encounter events or people who act as a mirror for us, it is another opportunity for us to resolve these emotions. When we consciously work on these emotions, we are once again placed in the situation that acts as a mirror for the unresolved conflicts within us – but now we confront the situation courageously and deal with it wisely, and those feelings may well disappear and leave our emotional body.

The mental body, and its conscious thoughts, has a certain influence on the astral body, but it is relatively minor. Just as the subconscious may create its system of laws and conventions, so the astral, emotional body works according to its laws. A very simple example may be seen in the person who repeatedly says that there is no reason to be afraid of the cockroach that is scuttling around on the floor. Only very rarely does this repetition have any practical effect on the person's fear. Intellectual thought has the ability to direct external behavior, but does not significantly affect the subconscious, except via various mantras of positive thinking that address the subconscious directly and change old patterns within it.

In the emotional body, we find all the old beliefs and emotional patterns that we have accumulated between childhood and maturity. Old wounds from our childhood reside there, as well as emotions of rejection, feelings of worthlessness, and various other non-positive patterns that we created about ourselves. These old patterns clash with our conscious world over and over again. A common conflict, for instance, is where a person yearns to love and be loved, but does not understand what is standing in his way. Why does love not burst into his life, or why does it repeatedly slip through his fingers? It is very likely that the unconscious belief that he is not worthy of love, or that he is incapable of love – a belief whose origin may date back to his early childhood, or even to his infancy – resides in his astral body.

However, this situation does not begin and end just in this life. Unresolved feelings, emotional conflicts, and their repercussions on our lives and on our surroundings (via our world-view and our conduct), continue with us into our subsequent incarnations, until they are resolved. This is because the emotional body does not disintegrate when the physical body dies, but continues into the next body, in the next incarnation. Moreover, a store of unresolved experiences is likely, to a great extent, to shape our next incarnation, and the conditions of our life in it.

When we assimilate these laws of the universe, we understand that in fact our fate is in our own hands. We cannot blame events, and certainly not other people, because we ourselves brought these events into our lives, be it via the emotional mass that is embodied in the emotional body during our present life, or be it in previous incarnations.

Most of the emotional complexes are located in the area of the solar plexus chakra. Via this chakra, we react emotionally to the experiences that occur in our lives. If we want to be conscious, in a rational way, of the emotions that are raging inside us, we have to stimulate the third eye chakra, which characterizes the highest form of expression of the astral body, so that we can penetrate the contents of the solar plexus chakra. However, even after the conscious understanding of the deep, and formerly unconscious, feelings that rage inside us, we have to open our hearts and change those patterns through conscious behavior. To this end, we need to stimulate and open the heart and crown chakras. When our heart is open, and universal wisdom directs and leads us, we can make the necessary repairs to this incarnation, and significantly influence the astral body. By directing the superego, we can begin to observe and understand the various experiences that we undergo, and what they are trying to teach us. Now we can learn life's lessons in a way that is not derisive, judgmental, or fearful, but rather understanding, learning, and repairing.

When the person's developed state of awareness and his connection to his superego for increasing periods of time cause the frequencies of his spiritual body to unite with his astral (emotional) body, the frequencies of his astral body become faster and faster. The faster they become, the more the astral body discards "bundles" of non-positive emotions, unresolved conflicts, and negative experiences. In this way, we slough off negative memories whose source is in negative experiences, and feel forgiveness and understanding toward ourselves and others. The more non-positive experiences are discarded, the more the frequencies of the astral body are fortified. It emits and radiates love, pity, compassion, joy, and gaiety to the environment, and attracts similar energetic vibrations to the person.

The mental (conceptual) body

The mental body is the third energetic body. All our ideas, rational thoughts, and even some of our intuitive perceptions are born in the mental body. It contains our thought patterns and mental beliefs, and is influenced by them. The vibrations of the mental body are higher than those of the ethereal and astral bodies, and its structure is less dense. It is also oval in shape, and it spreads over a distance of about 40-60cm from the body. The greater the person's awareness and conceptual and spiritual development are, the more space this body will occupy in the general electromagnetic field.

In cases where the person's conceptual development is relatively low, it is possible to discern the appearance of a kind of milky white substance in the person's mental body. In such cases, its colors will be relatively lacking in variety, faded, and dull. The more balanced, creative, original, and full of life and love the person's thoughts are, the more the colors of the aura of this body will be vivid, rich, and glowing.

The mental body has an upper layer and a lower layer. Its lower frequencies are expressed in linear thinking of the rational mind, which examines and checks what the eye can see using ostensibly logical equations. This layer is activated by thoughts concerning physical life, and by processing the information that is transmitted via the physical senses. The information is transmitted to the astral body via the ethereal body. The astral body translates the information into emotions, and transmits them in this form to the mental body. The mental body reacts to the information received through verbal thought, according to the patterns that are characteristic of the person.

The astral body and its emotions have a very strong influence on the apparently "rational" insight that is expressed in the conceptual body. Various emotional conflicts, unresolved emotional messes, affect the formation of thought, so that ultimately the majority of thought is neither objective nor "natural" – but rather the conceptual reaction to information expressed by the emotions according to understood thought patterns. The conceptual reaction is based on the way in which we react to the world, and can sometimes be different from the objective facts to which we relate. In addition, certain situations are liable to cause confusion in the astral body (which transmits the information to the mental body) so that the mental body cannot react properly. In such cases, the thought process becomes "confused" by the flood of various unconscious feelings. In these cases, we are likely to notice that when we are speaking to a person, he reacts to what we're saying in an emotional way that is not to the point.

Thoughts of this kind, which arise in the mental body, usually concern everyday matters and various material issues, and are linked to our general feeling and our more physical fields of interest. In this process, the main aim of the mental body is to supply rational answers and solutions to various opinions and information. However, this is only a minor use of the abilities of the mental body. The original use of this energetic body is to enable us to ask questions about universal truths, to assimilate them, and to "attract" information from the spiritual body – the mental body can absorb lofty insights and information. These insights, which come from the spiritual energetic body, are said to unite with rational thought in the mental layers by supplying the person with a more profound, objective, and conscious world-view. When this unity occurs, the person is able to react, both conceptually and practically, according to the laws of the universe. However, as we said before, in order to do this, the mental body's way of reacting has to be elevated so that it is less influenced by the unresolved emotional conflicts that reach it from the emotional layer along with the sensory information from the ethereal layer.

The mental layer contains all of our thought patterns. Often, we react according to these patterns, which are liable to be erroneous and irrelevant, instead of reacting rationally and objectively (which still does not constitute the highest use of the abilities of the mental body!). We must pay heed to the thought patterns that are stored in the mental layer. Located in this body are the beliefs, opinions, prejudices, and thought patterns (inhibiting ones, too) that we have accumulated during our lives. These thought patterns are projected outward, and, similar to what happens in the interaction between the universe and the astral layer, this situation also affects the reality in which we live. The beliefs to which we adhere in our thinking, attract situations and events that are compatible with this thought pattern. This is expressed in all areas of life.

Intensive work on recognizing thought patterns, creating awareness of the way of thinking, and altering inhibiting and useless thought patterns can be very helpful in many situations in the person's life. Working toward changing thought patterns that reside in the mental body is done by working on the subconscious: autosuggestion, hypnosis, and so on. Suggestions such as these work both on the mental body and on the astral body, which created them in the first place. This is not a trivial matter. As human beings, our path toward shaping our lives and our world begins and is rooted in thought. Physical embodiment in the material world and tangible reality begin in thought. Thought can stimulate speech, which is one of the main human ways of interacting, and after speech comes deed, which may make a karmic "repair" or, conversely, cause "damage." But everything begins in thought. Even things that are apparently done without thought ultimately derive from the astral (emotional) and the mental (conceptual) layers. This is because besides the conscious thoughts that go through our mind seemingly consciously and "voluntarily", there is an enormous mass of thoughts and emotional thoughts, inner beliefs, and conscious or unconscious thought patterns that actively direct our deeds.

When the person succeeds in discovering and identifying inhibiting thought patterns, and works on cleansing his astral body (which immediately affects his mental body), he may well begin to feel the full action of the mental body, which constitutes a link to the knowledge coming from the spiritual body.

The knowledge that comes to us from the spiritual body expresses itself as intuitive feelings, as inner enlightenment, as an insight, a sound or a vision. When the mental layer is healthy and balanced, it translates these intangible visions into conscious thought that can be expressed in speech. This brings the person to a deeper awareness and understanding of what is happening in his life. He sees a "passage" to simple linear thought, of cause and effect. His perception is broader and he can examine in depth the profound and fundamental factors that cause various events.

Reaching this layer – the higher layer of the mental body – necessitates the cleansing and understanding of the astral body with all the emotions contained in it, detaching oneself from old thought patterns and discarding them, and stimulating the third eye chakra by linking it to the crown chakra, which is open to receiving divine knowledge.

The spiritual (intuitive) body

The fourth conscious body is the spiritual body. It is also sometimes called the intuitive body, and some people call it or link it to the karmic body. The vibrations of this body are much higher than the vibrations of the other bodies, and it is the most subtle of all of them. In many people, this body is still undeveloped, or only partially developed. In people whose spiritual awareness is still undiscovered, the spiritual body does not extend a large distance from the physical body. In contrast, in a person who is spiritually developed and aware, the aura of the spiritual body may spread over a large distance, and its oval shape may turn into a perfect circle that encompasses the person with its light.

The spiritual body stores everything that is beyond what is defined as "rational", "logical", "cerebral." Through this body, the person receives intuitive messages, insights, and knowledge, and also experiences extrasensory perception and understanding, telepathic and prophetic dreams, "gut feelings," and prior knowledge.

The more balanced this body is, and the more aware and cognizant of it a person is, the easier it is to receive and decipher the intuitive messages that a person is receiving all the time, but is often unaware of. Alternatively, he may be aware of them, but he works against them.

It is possible to feel the spiritual body when we are in the presence of an enlightened, educated, just person, or true "maestro". When we are near him, we can feel a special feeling, which disappears when we move a certain distance away from him, leaving the area over which his aura extends. The feeling of these people's auras is a flow of love, peace, security, and tranquillity.

The aura of the spiritual body has a glowing and unique range of colors. This body frequently receives the highest energy, which, in order for it to be assimilated and understood, changes into lower frequencies that can be picked up by the mental, astral, and ethereal bodies. It makes itself compatible with the frequencies of these bodies, and helps them find the highest possible level of expression in their sphere. The way in which we receive, react, and store this energy depends on the state of our chakras.

Via the spiritual body, we experience a feeling of oneness with life, a feeling of connecting to God, to the universe, and to our fellow human beings, as well as to nature. When the person operates from his spiritual body, he acquires the ability to understand and access everything that exists in the universe.

This body is immortal. It is the divine part of us, while the other bodies are liable to change and even dissipate during our many incarnations.

Through the spiritual body, we can understand our objective in life, our vocation, and our existence in this world and in this incarnation. When connected to this conscious body, all of the person's actions stem from his higher self, and he operates perfectly according to the laws of the universe. Unconditional love flows in him, and affects his surroundings. Confidence, wisdom, power, and serenity accompany him constantly.

The spiritual body aspires, or is linked according to some people, to the additional body – the karmic body – about which very little is known. This body contains the knowledge concerning our vocation and the incarnations we have had, and our role as part of the universal whole.

The effects of the karmic body, or aura, are extremely important, but there aren't many people who know how to identify and understand them. They generally do so through channeling abilities, receiving superior messages, or the ability to discern the previous incarnations of the person, and the lesson he has to learn in this world and in this incarnation. Karmic effects are, for instance, handicaps, birth defects, serious deeds or crimes that are perpetrated against the person, severe mental illnesses, genetic diseases, perpetual poverty, and so on. Having said that, we have to remember the principle that everything is destined, but we do have freedom of choice. That means that despite the various karmic effects, the person can and must cope by balancing all his bodies; the aim of the karmic effects is to teach him how to cope with a certain situation in the most correct, connected, and pure way.

Because all the auras maintain a close interrelationship, a state of imbalance in one of the bodies has a direct effect on the other bodies. This point is very important when we set out to treat a particular disease or problem. Often, the physical problem can lead us to discover the basic imbalance that caused it, and is liable to continue creating situations of basic imbalance, until its root is treated. When we look at the problem holistically – that is, body, mind, and spirit together – we discover that in fact there is no "physical disease" or "mental disease" per se. Rather, every state of imbalance affects the various layers in one way or another, and is affected by them. When the person succumbs to a physical disease, or any other kind of disease, careful scrutiny reveals an imbalance in his other layers. In most cases, this imbalance is of the same type as the one that manifested itself physically. Often it is linked to the very chakra that affects both the particular mental state and the particular physical organs. In the same way, we can discover an imbalance in the various bodies, an imbalance that sometimes revolves around a certain point that will be manifested as some kind of physical disease in the physical body.

As an example, we will describe the possible source and development of a problem that is considered to be "easy" to describe from the point of view of its manifestation in the various layers. Constipation is a problem from which many people in the modern world suffer. It is clearly expressed in the physical body, and is liable to lead to many complications, such as excessive toxins in the digestive system, flatulence, chronically deficient digestion, and so on. When we examine the source of this disorder in the emotional-mental layer, we discover, theoretically, that constipation is an inability to let go. (This is in fact what happens in constipation!) It is possible that by looking at the person's characteristics, we will discover that he finds it difficult to let go of anything – money, possessions that he does not need, events from his past, and so on. When we observe his emotional behavior, we may see that he has difficulty letting go of emotions as well – he stops himself from expressing love, anger, or any other emotion, or finds it difficult to "let go" of various people in his life, and so on. If we observe his mental, conceptual behavior, we may see that he clings to old thought patterns that he "inherited" from his parents or from other people, and refuses to let go of them, although logically there is no point in clinging to them. This clinging to old, superfluous thought patterns is likely to be expressed in the intuitive layer as an inability to receive new knowledge and insights, to be open to various messages, or to heed his gut feeling, and in this way his intuitive abilities may be undermined. Of course, this is only an example (and each person must be related to individually by examining all of his problems and the properties of his personality and body), but it graphically demonstrates the interrelationship between our various bodies.

The problems, or imbalance, can start in any one of the bodies, but it is not easy to determine which preceded which – the chicken or the egg dilemma – if such "precedence" exists in the first place, since, as we said previously, the interrelationship is extremely close.

All of these problems, or states of imbalance or disharmony, constitute expressions of blockages in the person's bodies. In the same way as the blood, for instance, requires healthy, flexible arteries and veins in order for it to flow smoothly, so the flow of energy needs free and healthy "channels" without blockages. The correct flow of energy – a natural and smooth flow – will bring about balance on every level, and, of course, brings the person physical, mental, and spiritual health.

Free channels of energy are important and significant. When these channels are balanced, the person's ability to absorb and receive energy also depends on the balance and harmony between the bodies. When we observe the clever way in which we have been built, physically and energetically, in order to be a "vessel" or a "transmitter" of life energy (which is also called "chi") the question arises: What is the source of this energy that activates, affects, and realizes our being?

In the past, various philosophers tended to think, on the basis of mainly theoretical premises, that energy is located inside the person, and the person in fact constitutes a "closed circuit" from the energetic point of view, and nourishes and balances himself through his own self-energy. In contrast, many cultures, religions, and thinkers believe that the source of energy is in a tremendous energetic force that exists everywhere, all the time, and in everything.

Some people called this force "God", "The Great Spirit", "The Universal Force" and various other names, including attributing the source of energy to nature (which is also, of course, an embodiment of the universal force, or God). This force gives the person life, and affects his movement, exactly like it affects the movement of the stars and the spinning of the earth on its own axis, or the movement of atomic particles. This tremendous energy is what "seeps" into the inner being of the person, and the very fact of its being inside him makes him "divine" in a certain sense. This view, which is mainly based on spiritual experiments, as well as on scientific discoveries that describe it (albeit via different definitions), is the most accepted view among people who are involved with, see, or feel energies. The reason for this is simple: When the person develops the ability to observe the aura, he can often see how, in various situations, the person whose aura he is observing receives a "current" of energy of a certain shape from an external source. For instance, it is sometimes possible to see a line, sphere/s, or cone of light above the head of a person who is meditating, linked up, or praying.

In order to receive this energy, the person must be spiritually clean and pure, and feel a desire and deservedness to receive. He is supposed to (and deserves to) receive the exact "helping" of the energy that suits him at the given moment of his physical, mental, and spiritual development. Sometimes, people attempt to obtain more of this energy either by apparently materialistic expressions of "hoarding" or "accumulating" energy, or by attempts to draw more of the energy in its pure or more spiritual form. Drawing excessive amounts of energy by artificial means (such as drugs, for instance), is liable to cause a situation in which the person is unable to contain the amount of energy. The consequences can be negative or dangerous, exactly like getting an insufficient amount of energy is likely to manifest itself in various states of imbalance, such as fatigue, weakness, lack of vitality, and so on.

How is this energy channeled in a correct and harmonious way into our body, and how does the passage of energy and the connection between the various bodies work? We will find the answers further on in this book by understanding how the chakras operate.

Feeling the bodies

The various conscious bodies can be felt. Sometimes, feeling the bodies is done intuitively, through the development of spiritual awareness. It is also possible to do a few exercises to develop our ability to feel our energetic bodies – exercises that simultaneously strengthen the intuition and increase spiritual awareness.

Exercise 1: Sit or lie down comfortably. Ensure that your spine is straight. Relax all your muscles until you feel that your body is relaxed and calm. Start taking slow, comfortable, deep, abdominal breaths, while concentrating on releasing your body during exhalation. Begin to touch and feel your physical body. Feel your feet, your abdomen, pass your hands over your face, your chest, your knees. Feel your bones, the contact with your skin, your muscles. Go in deeper. in your mind's eye, and see yourself feeling your inner organs, which operate so harmoniously inside you. Using the power of your imagination, try to go in even deeper, and see in your mind's eye the cells and atoms that comprise you. Allow yourself some time to feel and see your physical body.

After a few minutes, begin to consciously connect to another part of you – your emotions. The emotions are not visible to the eye like the physical body and the external organs are, but can be felt in exactly the same way. Feel your emotions, the emotional energy that is in you now. What is the emotion that you are feeling? What is the feeling? In your imagination, bring up an irritating incident that happened recently. Imagine it in detail in front of your eyes. How do you feel? What feelings are you experiencing? How powerful are they? Ask yourself: How strong are the emotions at present (when you recall them) as opposed to their strength during the actual incident? Do you feel a difference? Connect to your physical body for a moment. How does your physical body feel when you imagine the irritating incident? Do you feel changes in your blood flow or in your muscle tension? Let the incident go; imagine it being cast into a distant sea, or any other place away from you. Calm down and relax your body.

Now see in your mind's eye a happy, moving, or exciting event that happened some time ago. Imagine all the details: the people, the smells, the sounds, the feeling that you experienced during those happy moments. Look inside yourself; how do you feel? What feelings and emotional energy are going through you? Connect to your physical body and feel how it reacts to the event. Do you feel an expansion in the heart or abdominal region? Are your mouth muscles being pulled upward? Breathe deeply and relax your body. You may feel a feeling of strength in your abdomen – power and action. Take a deep breath into your heart, feel how it opens, feel the tremendous love that is inside you, and let it flow and fill your entire being. These emotions exist inside you and around you all the time, even though you can't touch them physically.

After feeling the emotional body, close your eyes and begin to focus your attention on what's going on inside your head. Thoughts pass through; listen to them. Which thoughts are passing through your head? Listen to them attentively while they go through your head. Pay attention to how they pass, what their rate is. Are they "slippery," or are they "stable"? Do they come in a flood or in a trickle? What topics do they center on? You are capable of listening to your thoughts. Now, conduct an interesting experiment. Grab one of the thoughts and change it however you like. This is an amazingly simply process – but extremely powerful. You can observe your thoughts – therefore you are not your thoughts. You are a witness to them. You activate them and you can direct them. They do not control you; you can control them and direct them as you like.

Try and stay in this state of awareness for a few minutes. In this state, you are aware of your various bodies, you feel them, and you are a witness to them; notice that they are a part of you, and that you have the ability to intervene, control, and watch their actions.

Try to let the thoughts pass without relating to them or paying special attention to them. Try to remain relaxed, calm, and without thoughts for several minutes. Be aware of and attentive to the feelings that arise in you.

Practicing this exercise every now and then will help you reach a higher state of awareness of your conscious bodies, understand their action and the interrelationship between them, internalize your ability to control them, and take full responsibility for them.

Exercise 2: This is a very simple exercise for feeling the energy field, and develops the ability to feel the auric field and the energetic bodies. Despite its simplicity, it is very effective for strengthening the ability to feel energetically, and it is worthwhile practicing it until the natural sensation of feeling the aura becomes very easy. Sit comfortably. Take deep, slow breaths, and relax your body. Spread your arms out at your sides, and with a slow, circular movement, bring your arms toward each other, until they are 10-15cm apart. Begin to slowly move your palms near to each other and further apart, focusing on the sensation in them, without letting them touch, maintaining a distance of at least 7cm between them. When the energy field that surrounds each hand comes into contact with the energy field of the other hand, you will feel resistance, a magnetic feeling, or a slight prickling. These sensations are the "echoes" of the energetic action of the chakras in the hands.

Another way of doing the exercise is with a partner, when

both of you move your palms toward one another and further apart in order to feel the energy field that surrounds each one of them.

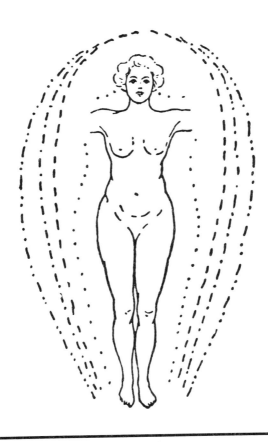

The chakras

The meaning of the Sanskrit word "chakra" is "wheel." Traditional writings relate that there are 88,000 chakras in the human being, which means that there is almost no area in the human body that is not energetically sensitive on a regular basis! By virtue of his very being, man is a creature that is tuned for frequent reception and conversion of energy. Most of the chakras are extremely small, with minor functions in the energy system. About 40 secondary chakras out of all the abovementioned ones have a significant function. The important ones among them are situated in the region of the spleen, the nape of the neck, the palms, and the soles of the feet.

The best-known and most significant chakras are the seven main chakras that are located along the central line of the body, parallel to the spine. These chakras play an extremely important role in human functions, in all layers of existence. They are responsible for the person's physical, mental, and spiritual functions.

These seven chakras are located in the ethereal body. Their shape is slightly reminiscent of that of a flower with petals and a stem, and in the ancient Hindu writings, they were described as similar to the lotus flower. The petals on the chakras represent energetic paths and channels through which the energy reaches the chakras, from where it goes to the subtle bodies. The number of petals changes from four on the base chakra to close to a thousand on the crown chakra.

From the center of each chakra, a leaf-like stem goes into the spine and joins with it. In this way, it connects the chakra with the most important energy channel, the Sushumana, which rises up along the spine to the head.

The chakras are in a state of perpetual rotation and vibration. Their rotation is what attracts and repels energy, according to the direction of the turn.

The chakras revolve in a clockwise direction, to the right, or in a counter-clockwise direction, to the left. A turn to the right has a yang, male meaning. It represents willpower and activity, and in its less positive meaning, aggressiveness and hunger for power. A turn to the left has a yin, female meaning, and symbolizes acceptance and acquiescence, as well as the less positive meaning, weakness.

It is important to recognize the direction in which the chakra turns in various types of treatment.

Every one of the chakras contains all the color frequencies, but there is one dominant color frequency that affects it, in accordance with the main action and function of the chakra. The more balanced the person's condition, and the higher his level of development and awareness, the stronger and brighter the color frequencies of the chakra. The size and vibrations of the chakras determine the amount of energy that they can absorb from various sources.

The chakras absorb energies that reach them from the universe, from nature, from celestial entities, from people, and even from things. They absorb and transmit energy to and from the various energetic bodies, and from the life-giving universal force.

The two most basic forms of energy reach the human system from the base chakra and the crown chakra. These two chakras are linked by the Sushumana, which is connected to the rest of the chakras by their "stems." Through the stems, it provides the chakras with essential energy. At the same time, the Sushumana is also the channel through which the Kundalini energy is stimulated.

When the Kundalini is stimulated, its energy is converted into various frequencies for each of the chakras, according to their frequencies, roles, and functions. The energy is manifested via the lowest frequencies of the base chakra, and the highest frequencies of the seventh chakra, the crown chakra. The converted frequencies are conveyed to the subtle bodies and to the physical body, and are perceived by us as sensations, emotions, and thoughts.

Each of the chakras is expressed on the physical body in one of the endocrine glands that regulate physical and emotional processes in the body. The higher energies, cosmic energies, are channeled through the chakras to the person's physical body. This energy, which is also called life energy, and flows through the chakras, is of cardinal importance to our lives and physical, mental and spiritual health.

When a situation arises in which the energy does not flow harmoniously through the chakras, or when one of the chakras is blocked or open too wide, it results in an imbalance that is manifested in all areas of life. The imbalance in the chakra will also be expressed in the endocrine gland that is linked to it, and the delicate metabolic balance of the body will be upset.

All the conscious bodies (that we mentioned previously), as well as the material body and everything else that exists in the universe, have their own unique vibrational frequency. Ideally, all of the person's conscious bodies are supposed to be linked and connected harmoniously. If one of the conscious bodies is not linked to one of the other bodies, it will prevent the passage of information and energy between those bodies. For instance, when the mental (conceptual) body and the emotional body are disconnected, the person may be unable to express his thoughts, or his emotions. Like any other sophisticated "instrument," which works on the principle of receiving and giving (absorption and transmission), the person also needs centers for absorption, transmission, and conversion of energy. These centers are the chakras.

In the physical body, the chakras function as "transmitters." They transmit the currents that arrive from the higher, purer energy, which operates at higher frequencies of the energetic bodies, to the physical body, by "converting" the high frequency to a frequency that our physical body can utilize. In the same way that domestic use of electrical energy that is too high (that is, at a different voltage) is liable to cause a short circuit, so the non-conversion of the energy that operates at higher frequencies in people can cause a blockage.

The conscious body that absorbs and contains the person's soul is the spiritual conscious body, which is our divine side, and it links us to creation. From this body, the energy passes to the other conscious bodies, each of which has a different objective and vocation. For this reason, each conscious body requires energy of a different quality and frequency. On each "surface" there are stations that convert the energy for the next surface.

The entire universe is connected by a tremendous primeval force. This force is transmitted to every thing and creature according to its capacity, and in accordance with the frequencies that suit it from the physiological, emotional, intellectual, and spiritual points of view. When the energy makes its way from this vast, primeval force to the bodies that are located in the universe, its strength and power apparently decrease more and more, so that these bodies can absorb it (since they cannot tolerate even an iota of its full original strength).

The human body, and the universe as well, is built of different layers – a spiritual layer, an emotional layer, an intellectual layer, and of course a material layer. The difference between the human body and the "body" of the cosmos lies only in the length of their waves and frequencies. As a result, the divine force is found not only outside us, but also inside us. Since human beings are able to use the gift of the imagination, they can attune themselves intellectually, intuitively, or emotionally, to the various energetic bodies and the various layers of awareness, and change them. All the methods of expanding consciousness, such as positive thinking, guided imagery, meditation, and many others, do this.

Consciousness is a very powerful tool. It is not limited by matter, distance, or time, and can move within our multidimensional being via the different layers of awareness. These changes can occur frequently and quickly. For this reason, the body's energy centers are very important. Every chakra serves as a relay and transmitting station to a particular area of frequency or awareness. When attention is focused on one of the chakras, the person is mainly involved in fields for which the particular chakra is "responsible," consciously or unconsciously. Often, this can help us diagnose a problem or an imbalance in one of the chakras. The person is liable to manifest deficient functioning in a field that is clearly connected to the action of one or more of the chakras. He is likely to talk about this at length, focus on it, and even display emotional and physical signs that lead us to identify the deficient functioning of one of the chakras.

Concentrating on the problem does not help solve it – on the contrary. The greater the amount of energy invested in thought and emotion concerning the problem itself, the more the problem will grow, or stagnate. In contrast, concentrating on balancing the chakra itself will lead to the opposite – positive – results: balancing the chakra and correcting the general imbalance (physical, emotional, and spiritual) that stemmed from the chakra's deficient functioning.

Through their spiritual abilities, the rishis (sages) of ancient India received information about the human energy system. They wrote this information in vedas that contain ancient knowledge. In India, as in other ancient, enlightened cultures, the chakras are aligned to certain colors, elements, signs, and properties. The combination of these elements – for instance, looking at a particular shape in a particular color while saying a mantra that is attributed to a particular chakra – that are linked to the chakra creates a certain frequency that can link up to a certain element in the human body via a certain resonance. For example, the element of earth is linked to the sex glands, to the first chakra, to the planet Mars, to the color red, and to the ruby. This technique of combining the elements leads to general balance that positively affects the person.

This activity also works in the opposite direction. When a person focuses on a certain property, desire, or aspiration, allows it to control his life, and lives by it, a situation arises wherein he works, lives, and communicates more from within the chakra that is linked to the subject to which he attributes so much importance. This is a "chicken or egg" situation in which a certain perception, way of thinking, and way of behaving causes an imbalance in the chakras. This imbalance, in turn, is liable to cause the situation to become extreme. It is difficult to say whether the imbalance in the chakra is what caused the imbalance in behavior, thought, and emotion, or vice versa.

We can look at a common example of this imbalance. A person whose entire focus of interest is increasing his income and accumulating more and more money, property, and assets, spends the greater part of his days concentrating on everyday problems, material issues, and physical matters without paying any attention to his intellectual, mental, or spiritual development.

This person's awareness is significantly concentrated on his first chakra, and most of his thoughts are focused on survival, safeguarding his income, and materialistic issues. When most of the person's thoughts focus on a particular chakra in an unbalanced way, this can be expressed in several ways. For instance, excessive concentration on the first chakra is liable to characterize a person with violent impulses and a lust for wealth or sex – and conversely, this powerful energy is likely to express itself in strong energies, in a powerful life force, in a celebration of life, and great vitality. Thus, concentration on a particular chakra, which ultimately creates a certain imbalance, can be expressed in many different ways, according to the development of the personality. In the same way, the colors of the chakra, which are expressed in the aura, can change. In the above example, the color of the first, or base, chakra can appear in different shades of red, from dark, "dirty" red, which indicates extreme materialistic behavior, or addiction to drugs or alcohol, to bright, "clean" red, which can be indicative of a sensitive person who copes with his surroundings well, but is mainly interested in materialistic matters.

This situation is likely to be repeated in the other chakras, and of course, will be manifested in the colors of the whole aura. The more a person focuses on one aspect of life and awareness, such as creativity, materialism, mental development, spiritual development, and so on, the more this will be expressed in the activity of the chakra that is responsible for this field. This affects the state of the other chakras too, because of their interrelationship, as well as all the person's fields of awareness and existence, and his conscious bodies. When a strong frequency of a certain color is seen in the aura – yellow, for instance – it shows that most of the person's consciousness is focused on the solar plexus chakra. This may indicate sensitivity in the stomach. It may also indicate much greater concentration on the activities of the third chakra – for example, the desire to be freer or independent and uncommitted. These attempts, which focus on the action of the third chakra, are projected onto the entire aura and make the yellow into the dominant color at that time.

The conscious bodies are linked to the aura, to the electromagnetic field, via the chakras. According to the colors of the person's aura, it is possible to know if his awareness is located more in the physical, mental, spiritual, or intellectual layer, and if there is some kind of imbalance between these areas and the action of the chakras.

The petals and stems of the chakras

A linking energetic thread of subtle energetic matter flows through the crown chakra and penetrates the physical body. It passes in a straight line from the head to the perineal area (the point that is located between the genitals and the anus). Every chakra has "petals" and a "stem." The stems of the crown and base chakras are open and *integral to* the central energetic thread. The rest of the chakras are located along this energetic thread. They have petals that open into the anterior part of the aura field, and stems that radiate into the posterior part of the aura field. Most of the stems remain closed, but the petals are flexible, and open and close like the petals of a flower. They move, open, and close according to the various life situations and feelings we experience. When the chakra is flexible, and can open and close like the petals of a flower, it is healthy. This flexibility is not a given. There could be situations in which the flexibility of the chakra is not optimal. It becomes rigid, the energies do not flow properly, and ultimately, the chakra, in such a situation, can become blocked.

Blocked chakras are not rare. These blockages can be caused by various things – generally by long-term processes. A severe or cumulative trauma, too, that affects a particular chakra, is liable to cause it to lose its flexibility or to become blocked relatively quickly. An extreme example of this is a rape, which can seriously affect the sexual chakra. An immediate blockage may occur, and this affects all the areas of the victim's life. There can also be a gradual hardening of the chakra, in which the chakra becomes blocked as a result of the attack. Having said this, except for severe traumas, the process of loss of flexibility of the chakra and its loss of the ability to open and close according to the situations of life is generally gradual and lengthy.

We can compare the action of the healthy chakra to that of a valve. It closes when necessary, and opens as need be. It does not open up to unwanted energy or to a negative reaction, but lets it flow over it without filtering it inside. In contrast, it can open itself up to suitable and correct energy. So it is possible to see the importance not only of the opening of the chakra, but also of its ability to close when necessary.

These marvelous capabilities of the chakras can be disrupted, as we said, by severe traumas, but there are additional factors that affect the chakras: regular use of drugs and medications, excessive intake of alcohol and tobacco, and regular or prolonged use of medical anesthesia. After a local or general anesthetic, the chakras require immediate treatment and balancing.

These situations can cause the chakras to remain open – resulting in the person being extremely vulnerable and sensitive to external influences – or to cause them to harden gradually and close, so that the person loses certain abilities and sensations that derive from the action of a particular chakra.

These situations can be treated by healing and color therapy (to which the chakras respond wonderfully). However, most of the work on the chakras is self-treatment, which includes awareness, visualization – especially of color and movement – and conscious breathing.

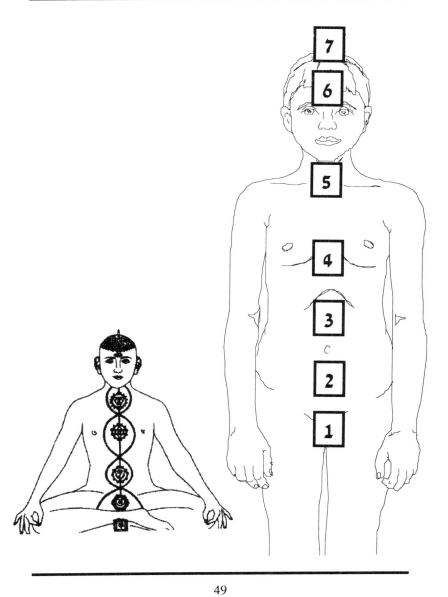

The first chakra

The base (root) chakra

Muladhara

Location of the chakra: In the region of the perineum – the point located between the genitals and the anus.

Colors: Red and black.

Complementary color: Blue.

Symbol: A circle surrounded by four lotus petals, with a square inside it. Sometimes, the square is colored yellow-gold, which symbolizes the material world, and it can contain the letters of the sound or mantra "lam." A stem emerges from the square, symbolizing the chakra's link to the central thread, the Sushumana.

Key words: Deep-rootedness, stability, acceptance, self-preservation, survival, perception.

Basic principles: Physical willpower for existence and survival.

Inner aspect: Being grounded.

Energy: Vitality.

Age of development: From birth to between three and five years.

Element: Earth.

Sense: Smell.

Sound: "Lam."

Body: The physical body.

Nerve plexus: Coccyx.

Hormonal glands linked to the chakra: Sexual and adrenal glands.

Body organs linked to the chakra: The "hard" organs

of the body – the spine, the skeleton, the bones, teeth, and nails. The excretory organs – the anus, the rectum, the intestines. The birth and reproductive organs – the prostate glands and the gonads. Also, the blood and the cell structure.

Problems and diseases that occur during an imbalance of the chakra: Constipation, hemorrhoids, fatigue, apathy, lack of energy, blood problems, problems of stress in the spine, joint and bone problems, problems in the tissues, and skin problems.

Essential oils: Patchouli, cedarwood, sandalwood, vetiver.

Crystals and stones: Agate, ruby, onyx, hematite, red jasper, bloodstone, red coral, cuprite, garnet, jet, rhodochrosite, spinel, smoky quartz, alexandrite, black tourmaline.

Stars and astrological signs linked to the chakra: The base chakra is symbolized by the planets Mars, Pluto, and Saturn, and the signs of Aries, Taurus, Scorpio, and Capricorn.

Aries, the first sign of the Zodiac, symbolizes a new beginning, primeval life energy, power, and aggressiveness.

Taurus symbolizes the affinity for nature and earth, stability, passion, and the pleasures of the senses.

Scorpio symbolizes sexual power, transmutation, and renewal.

Capricorn symbolizes stability, gradual activity, and structuralism.

The base chakra, which is also called the root chakra, is located in the region of the perineum. Its petals point downward, toward and between the legs, and its stem points upward, toward the central thread – the Sushumana. In a healthy and natural state, it should be slightly open.

This chakra is our link to the material world. It conveys cosmic energies to our physical and earthly layers, and causes the stabilizing earth energy to flow into the energetic bodies. The base chakra is exactly what its name suggests. It constitutes the basis for the activity of the rest of the chakras, and for our existence, constitution, and development. It grounds us to the earth by safeguarding the nourishing and life-giving link with this source of power. It grants us a feeling of confidence and stability, which we need for our development on all levels. We are energetic creatures, and our souls are immortal, but when we come into this world, by dint of the karmic law that decrees that we have to go through various incarnations in order to repair our karma, we become part of the earth element that gives life to our physical body and nourishes it. The more securely we feel our roots embedded in the earth, the easier and simpler our physical lives in the material world become.

The base chakra stimulates our basic survival instinct – the need to work toward stability, which provides us with food, shelter, a family, and continuity, all of which are part of our role and needs in this world. Moreover, it is this chakra that activates the sexual instincts (as opposed to the *awareness* of sexuality, which is one of the functions of the second chakra). The sexual instinct is embedded in this chakra because of the need for continuity and self-preservation by creating an additional "shoot" from the basic trunk.

The base chakra represents the struggle for survival and self-preservation, and it is the source of all the instincts that exist in order to protect ourselves and safeguard our physical and mental health, as well as fulfill our basic needs. First and foremost – the "instinctive" desire and aspiration to protect ourselves against danger. Fears that prevent us from getting into a situation that can jeopardize our physiological or mental health are part of the self-protective mechanism that is activated by this chakra. Most of these fears are basic, and shared by all human beings, such as the fear of falling, of fire, of drowning, and so on. Various conditions of life – mainly competitive ones – cause the person to test the limits of these primal fears. In general, people do not put these basic fears to the test unless there is a desperate need to do so, or they are motivated by a competitive impulse and a need to prove their abilities. These are manifestations of a situation of imbalance in this chakra, often involving an unbalanced solar plexus chakra. Cases of imbalance in the survival instincts of the base chakra can lead to cowardice and dependence on the judgment and opinions of others – and, on the other hand, to going to extremes and taking exaggerated risks.

Harmonious functioning of the base chakra

When the base chakra is open and operates harmoniously, the person feels a deep and direct connection to the earth and to the life forms in nature. He feels grounded in a positive way, connected to life, and full of interest. He feels stability, self-satisfaction, and inner strength. He is assertive, and can cope with conflicts and crises courageously. He can make decisions and act on them without any real difficulties; he is energetic, active, and discerning; he has healthy sexuality and a strong life force.

When the chakra is balanced, the person feels that the cyclical nature of the universe is perfectly natural, because this is the chakra that symbolizes new beginnings, ends, and cyclicality. The person feels the desire to shape his life himself, and build it, taking nature and the earth into account. Accomplishing material objectives is relatively easy, and he feels confidence in the universe and in the course of life. This feeling of confidence prevents worry about basic survival needs, because he feels that everything he requires can be found in the world and will be supplied to him. Moreover, when the base chakra is well balanced and open, the person can link the spiritual layers of the universe to the basic material actions of life on earth. This situation creates spirituality that is not "up in the clouds", but rather is expressed in all the person's moves and actions. He may feel that his head is in the clouds while his feet are firmly planted on the ground.

Unharmonious functioning of the base chakra

An imbalance in the base chakra is manifested in a disproportional focus on survival and material needs. All of the person's thoughts and interests are focussed on physical needs such as food, drink, sex, and money. These are likely to take first priority, and occasionally, in severe states of imbalance, to constitute the peak of his aspirations or his main source of interest. The person is liable to feel the need to satisfy his lusts without taking the consequences of his actions into account, because of a powerful and tangible urge to gratify these needs quickly. This state of imbalance of the chakra is likely to be expressed in sexual promiscuity and sexual imbalance. Moreover, the person may feel that he is unable to give or receive freely, either in material or emotional matters. He may focus partially or entirely on satisfying his needs, while ignoring the needs and feelings of other people. The greed for money is liable to take control of him, followed by the need to accumulate more and more material assets (which is never satisfied – somewhere deep down there is always a feeling of instability and a lack of confidence in the universe).

When the chakra is not balanced, various existential fears may emerge: fears of lack, of poverty, of physical deterioration, and so on, as well as severe anxieties. The person may be very "earthy" in the non-positive connotation of the word, to the point that matters that are not absolutely physical will be difficult for him to comprehend. People whose base chakra is not balanced are likely to be extremely egocentric, aggressive, and short-tempered. They may try to impose their will and opinions on others by force or aggressiveness, and feel rage, anger, or even violence when their desires are not fulfilled.

The connection between the base chakra and the physical body

Every one of the chakras affects and is affected by the physical body, its functioning, and its health. This connection is mainly manifested in the action of the glands. Each of the chakras, *with the exception of the base chakra*, is linked to one of the subtle bodies.

The base chakra, with the lowest frequency, is connected to the physical, solid body, and to the most "solid" aspects of the body – the bones, skeleton, flesh, muscles. When situations of imbalance occur in these basic organs, the state of the base chakra must be examined.

Treatment of the chakra, and work with aromatic oils, crystals, colors, and various physical and psychological techniques, will lead to an improvement in the physiological condition by balancing the chakra and opening its blockages. Thus, these treatments can help with problems such as rheumatism, arthritis, and other joint and bone, tissue, and skin problems.

One of the symptoms that can indicate problems in the base chakra is the feeling of a lack of love – or even revulsion – toward one's body and its basic functions (such as a feeling of disgust toward our excretory organs, etc.). When the base chakra is properly balanced, the person knows his body, appreciates it, and accepts all of its functions naturally. A healthy base chakra inspires a feeling of appreciation toward the physical body, with its variety of marvelous and enjoyable activities. A feeling of physical power is built up inside us, the ability to move ourselves and use and activate our body as we like. However, a lack of appreciation for the body, or contempt for our physical layers, as well as for our physical needs such as eating, physical activity, excretion, motion, or sexual activity, requires an investigation of the state of the base chakra, and balancing it, if necessary.

When the base chakra is blocked or unbalanced, physical disorders in the organs linked to the chakra may occur – in the spine, skeleton, bones, legs, teeth, nails, sphincter, intestines, blood, prostate gland, and gonads.

Our back and spine represent the feeling of support that we experience, ostensibly externally – but we must remember that everything we experience "outside" of ourselves is a reflection of our feelings toward ourselves. States of imbalance in the base chakra are generally characterized by some kind of feeling of a lack of external support – a lack of support by those around us, which is always a mirror that reflects the support we give ourselves; or a feeling of a lack of support by the universe, which is expressed in a fear of the future, of a lack of money, of accidents, and so on. Since these feelings are so common, and many people feel that they have to "fight" for their lives in our current apparently competitive world, many people suffer constantly from back pains and slipped disks that stem from similar causes.

Two additional problems that are very characteristic of an unbalanced base chakra are constipation and hemorrhoids. Constipation symbolizes a basic problem in the ability to let go. Although it is very common, it should not be treated lightly. Constipation can lead to numerous complications, among them excessive toxins in the digestive system, flatulence, chronically deficient digestion, and so on. As we said previously, constipation symbolizes an inability to let go. This can be expressed in various behaviors: difficulty in letting go of money – stinginess; difficulty in releasing feelings – either in expressing them or in the inability to let go of past hurts; hoarding old things; maintaining relationships that are no longer supportive, and so on. On the mental, conceptual layer, this is likely to stem from the inability to let go of old, useless, and inhibiting thought patterns. When there is a problem of chronic constipation, it requires immediate treatment. It is not a "minor" problem, as people are inclined to think. In cases of chronic constipation that extend over long periods in the person's life, the root of the problem could lie in the age of development of the base chakra – some time between the ages of one and five, approximately. In any event, it is necessary to perform a deep balancing of the base chakra in order to solve the problem.

Sphincter problems also represent different layers of difficulty in letting go. The idea of difficulty in releasing often stems from the feeling of "I don't have, I won't have, if they take it away from me, I won't have anything," and so on. This is indicative of a basic lack of confidence in the universe, an inability to adjust oneself to the cyclical nature of nutrition and getting rid of waste products – excretion, letting go. Hemorrhoids also represent the fear of letting go – often of hurts that occurred in the past. They can also constitute the physical pattern of an emotional fear that there isn't enough time. Moreover, a lack of confidence in the universe – that it will provide us with everything we need, when we need it – lies at the root of the problem.

The base chakra is also linked to the bones and joints. The bones represent structure, basis. When the perception of the basis is shaky, it means that the person does not feel in harmony with the structure of the universe and its processes. The bones can suffer from different problems, and may sometimes indicate general states of imbalance and proper grounding. Scoliosis, which occurs in many people at the onset of adolescence and slightly prior to that, represents the same feeling of a lack of support by the universe, a lack of confidence in its processes, and an inability to flow with them harmoniously. Although it appears during adolescence, it generally develops during the preceding years, and only manifests itself later on. The way in which we grasp the universe's support of us – flowing with us rather than "against" us – is embedded in the first years of the chakra's development, and traumas at this age affect the general amount of confidence we have in life.

The joints, which move our limbs, represent flexibility and the ability to accept changes, which cannot be done harmoniously without a solid basis and a starting point from which we can keep on shaping our lives as we wish. Various joint problems, such as rheumatism and arthritis, require that the condition of the base chakra be checked and balanced immediately.

Blood is also linked to the action of the base chakra. Blood is the essence of life, the essence of the physical body. A negative approach toward the various layers of life, hostility in its various forms, and a lack of happiness, deriving from an inability to understand the nature of our existence in the physical world, can lead to anemia and problems in coagulation of the blood.

The influence of the chakra on hormonal activity

The base chakra is linked to the gonads and to the adrenal glands. The gonads (the testicles in men and the ovaries in women) are part of the endocrine system. The hypophysis (in the brain) is the gland that oversees the action of the gonads "from above." At its hormonal command, hormones are released and various processes occur in the testicles and ovaries. The action of the gonads is necessary for performing some of the most basic functions of the base chakra: continuity, fertility, and maintaining the sexual instinct and its proper functioning.

When there are any problems in the functioning of the gonads and we diagnose sexual impotence caused by a hormonal or physiological source, as well as sterility, we have to examine the base chakra. In such cases, we treat, balance, and open the chakra, as well as use projections of the color red, and red stones. The color red stimulates the sexual layers into action, and helps in the treatment of impotence and sterility. A survey of the crystals and stones that are suitable for the base chakra reveals that many of them act in the same way. The aromatic oils that are suitable for work with the base chakra are likely to be very helpful in solving problems linked to the gonads and sexuality – fertility and instinctive sexuality, that is, sexual potency.

The adrenal glands clearly represent part of the most basic functions of the base chakra. They are located above the upper lobe of the kidneys and consist of an outer layer that produces steroid (fatty) hormones, and an inner layer that produces a protein hormone. Among the hormones that are secreted by the outer adrenal layer, it is important to mention aldosterone, which participates in the regulation of blood pressure by influencing the kidney, and works at keeping water and salts in the body, as well as cortisol, which is very important when there is an injury or an acute disease. Cortisol increases the amount of foodstuffs (glucose, amino acids, and fatty acids) in the blood, thus enabling the body to cope better with situations of stress. These two hormones are essential for life. Cortisol is an energetic generator, and is also responsible for storing energy, and regulates the element of fire in the body. Aldosterone, as we said, prevents the loss of fluids and maintains the balance between potassium and sodium in the body.

The inner adrenal layer secretes the hormone adrenaline into the bloodstream during states of mental or physical stress. The physical changes that adrenaline causes enable the body to cope better with situations of stress. Through this mechanism, the "fight or flight" response is activated. This response occurs in situations of stress, and was originally a primitive mechanism from the early stages of evolution, and was meant to prepare the body for battle or rapid flight in a life-threatening situation. We still have this mechanism. Today, when real life-threatening situations are relatively rare, it is activated in a variety of stress situations. In such situations, the adrenaline operates in parallel to the sympathetic nervous system and both mechanisms exert a similar effect on the organs. The adrenaline that is secreted causes an increase in heart and lung capacity, a broadening of the respiratory tract, a reduction of the blood flow to the skin, increased perspiration, an increase of the blood supply to the muscles, dilation of the pupils, and so on. All these reactions prepare the person for quick and immediate action. When the person is perpetually in situations of stress, this reaction will be activated repeatedly, thus causing an excessive use of the adrenaline supply, draining it faster than it can be replenished. Thus, the person may succumb to conditions of physical exhaustion and even collapse, and will require a great deal of rest and treatment in order to recover.

Situations of stress and tension are individual and relative. As real life-threatening situations are rare today, there should not be many reasons for activating this reaction. This is not the case, however. Many people tend to get stressed out for various reasons, and sometimes activate this reaction on a daily basis – while driving, at work, during a meeting with the boss, facing a deadline, in domestic arguments, coping with study and exam pressures, financial pressures, and many more reasons. Situations of stress that activate the "fight or flight" mechanism, constitute one of the main factors in weakening the immune system, as well as the functioning of the entire body. When the base chakra is balanced, and the person feels that life is supporting him, the chances of erosive activation of the adrenal glands are smaller. (The state of the solar plexus chakra is also very important, as it also affects the adrenal glands, and in a balanced state affords awareness and control of the various situations of stress.)

The second chakra

The sexual chakra

Swaddhisthana

Location of the chakra: On the pelvis, between the pubic bones.

Color: Mainly orange, but also yellow leaning to orange.

Complementary color: Blue.

Symbol: A circle surrounded by five or six lotus petals. Sometimes another circle appears inside the first circle, containing the letters of the sound "vam." A stem emerges from the circle, symbolizing the chakra's link to the rest of the chakras and to the force of the universe. Sometimes a silver-gray half-crescent appears in the circle.

Key words: Change, sexuality, creativity, feeling of the other, honesty, inner strength, confidence.

Basic principles: Creative reproduction of the being.

Inner aspect: Emotions, sex.

Energy: Creation.

Age of development: Between the ages of three and eight.

Element: Water.

Sense: Touch and taste.

Sound: "Vam."

Body: Ethereal body.

Nerve plexus: Sacrum.

Hormonal glands linked to the chakra: The gonads – ovaries, testicles – the prostate gland and the lymphatic system.

Body organs linked to the chakra: The pelvis, the lymphatic system, the kidneys, the bladder, the muscles, the genitals, and all the body fluids: blood, lymph, digestive juices, semen.

Problems and diseases that occur during an imbalance of the chakra: Muscle spasms, allergies, physical frailty, constipation, sexual imbalance and lack of libido, sterility, inhibitions and repressions, lack of creativity.

Essential oils: Rosemary, rose, ylang-ylang, juniper, sandalwood, jasmine.

Crystals and stones: Amber, citrine, topaz, moonstone, fire agate, orange spinel, fire opal.

Stars and astrological signs linked to the chakra: The sexual chakra is symbolized by the moon, the planets Venus and Pluto, and the signs of Libra, Cancer, and Scorpio.

Libra symbolizes relationships that are based on partnership and equality, sensuality, creativity, and attention to the self.

Cancer symbolizes wealth of feelings, fertility, and acceptance.

Scorpio symbolizes sexual passion, sensuality, and transmutation by foregoing the ego in sexual unity.

The sexual chakra is also called the sacral chakra, and its Sanskrit name is Swaddhisthana. It is located on the pelvis, and its petals are approximately two finger-widths below the navel. Its stem reacts to the region of the sacrum and its nerve plexus.

The sexual chakra is the center for unfiltered primeval emotions, the sexual energies, and creativity. It symbolizes change and individuality through understanding the uniqueness of the other.

The energies of the sexual chakra are drawn from the base chakra and mingle with them. When the base chakra is properly balanced, stable, and established, it gives the sexual chakra confidence. When the principle of confidence is not balanced and anchored in the base chakra, this will affect the sexual chakra and its attributes. In such cases, the person may feel a lack of confidence toward himself and his abilities, but mainly toward the world around him.

Another of the most important functions of this chakra stems from the confidence the person feels toward the world: the feeling of the other. The meaning of this feeling is to include the other in our feelings, interests, and thoughts, in the same way as a mother feels toward her child, but according to the specific relationship. When the chakra is balanced, and it draws confidence from the base chakra, we can experience the other separately from ourselves, but simultaneously, as a part of us. We are sensitive and caring toward life around us, empathetic toward other people's feelings, considerate of them, of their desires, and of their emotions. All this happens when we feel like an independent and non-dependent whole, an individual. This attitude is acquired in the earliest days of childhood, and is affected by the way the parents relate to the child, and the way the environment relates to him. When the chakra is not balanced, a lack of caring about others can arise as a result of too much focus on oneself, or a state of dependency, or even a symbiotic relationship, when the person does not know where he ends and the other begins.

The sexual chakra is the center for sexuality, for sexual pleasure, including the awareness of fertility and sexual desire. As opposed to the base chakra, which is responsible for sexual instincts only, the sexual chakra is responsible for the broader sense of sexuality. The sexual chakra relates directly to the sexual act itself, and also to the manner in which we perceive our sexuality, to our acceptance of the gender into which we were born. It includes the way we accept and perceive ourselves as men or women while relating to social norms – taking into account the particular ages and periods of our lives. It is responsible for the awareness of sexuality, sexual choice, and the mass of emotions and associations that are connected with sex. Our sexual patterns are located in this energetic center, as are various patterns that have been imprinted on us by society. It is this chakra that absorbs the norms concerning sex and the attitude to sex that is prevalent in the young child's surroundings, whether they are norms of acceptance, naturalness and beauty, or feelings of sin and prohibition. The various beliefs regarding the man's "function" or the woman's "function" from the sexual and relationship points of view are "absorbed" into this chakra.

The sexual chakra is the seat of the ability to create, produce, give birth – producing something new and leaving a personal stamp. It is the seat of change, which is joined by curiosity, adventure, and innovation. Change and accepting change constitute a fundamental element in the development of the awareness – the ability to ask questions, not cling to what exists, to investigate and inquire about the unknown and the new. These are also the foundations of creativity.

The sexual chakra is also responsible for our creative organs – the organs that give life to a new person, to a newborn baby, whose personality and being express his parents – physically, genetically, and mentally – on the one hand, and his individuality and state of being a separate entity on the other. This is creation – any creation. It is born in the person's innermost being, but the moment it is externalized, it has a life of its own.

The second chakra is the one that channels our inner abilities outward, and activates our inner strength, which is manifested in the ability to turn ideas into reality, to "activate" raw potential and turn it into something concrete – exactly like the child is raw potential when he is sperm and ovum, then a fetus in his mother's womb, and becomes a perfect, real being when he is born. The significance of inner strength is the ability to express our uniqueness, to realize our potential without being afraid of other people's reactions, without asking for permission and acquiescence, and using our talents fearlessly. This process is profoundly linked to the ability to recognize our power, and not to hand it over to others.

When we let others – who may be our parents, our surroundings, our mate, the "norms," the government, or any other factor – determine our personal attributes for us, and repress our inner feelings, beliefs, and abilities, we "hand over" to them the strength that is within us, because we forego its realization. This does not mean, of course, that these factors will take it from us by force. It is a question of giving inner permission to other people, out of a need for confirmation and acceptance, to judge us, to manipulate us, to persuade us to act in ways that are alien to us, possibly by smooth talking us.

People tend to consent to this because of the need to "be like everyone else." But this is exactly the nature of the second chakra: the ability to "be like everyone else," to be a "part," without relinquishing our individuality and uniqueness, which are expressed directly in our unique way of thinking, our beliefs, and our feelings.

Often, people allow various factors, near or far, to force their negative influence on them and to affect their mature choice, because of this need to be part of society, and because of the fear of being ostracized. When the person is well aware of his inner strength, and his self-esteem and self-acceptance are strong, he does not permit manipulations of this type, and does not surrender his individuality for the sake of social acceptance. In contrast, he will respect the wisdom, experience, and talents of others, and will feel that they are giving him, teaching him, and reinforcing his personal strength through their ways of teaching. Having said that, he will not let the strength of human beings blind him, nor turn them into "gurus" at whose feet he surrenders the individuality of his being. States of imbalance in the sexual chakra can seriously affect the person's ability to stand up for himself and to adhere faithfully to the personal path that leads to self-fulfillment.

However, individuality does not mean turning one's back on society – on the contrary. When the sexual chakra is properly balanced, the person feels like an active partner in the shaping of his family, his community, and the society in which he lives, and aspires to function in it out of a desire to improve it and bring peace and tranquillity. The sexual chakra symbolizes the apparent duality of the wish to maintain our individuality but to be part of the whole. This duality, in fact, doesn't exist, because by being whole and perfect entities we are part of the universe in body, soul, and spirit. The changes that occur in the world affect these layers, directly or indirectly. Because we are energetically linked to our human brethren, to the earth, and to every form of life that exists there, we are responsible and influential, and we are also influenced by the changes in the universe.

When the person can live in peace both with his unique self, and everything that this involves, and with his surroundings and society, he can be honest. Honesty, both with himself and with his surroundings, is one of the functions for which the sexual chakra is responsible. Honesty is freedom from fear and anxiety. When the second chakra is well-balanced, the person can first and foremost be honest with himself. In many situations, human beings agree to delude themselves, to "turn a blind eye," to deceive themselves, for a variety of reasons. Many of these reasons stem from a lack of confidence in the universe. When the person is not sure that the universe looks out for him like a beloved child, or like an only child, many fears and anxieties about the future, about the other, creep in and take control of his soul. This leads to the person being unable to be honest with his surroundings. A lack of honesty stems from fear – the fear that telling, acting, and even thinking the truth will somehow lead to the person being hurt. When a person is confident of his inner strength, he is aware that nothing in the world can harm his soul if he expresses its truths.

Harmonious functioning of the sexual chakra

When the sexual chakra operates harmoniously, it expresses itself in vital and emotional movement in all areas of life. The person feels that he is an individual, recognizes his self, but is open to and accepts the feelings of others, and can connect to them easily. He connects to members of the opposite sex easily, and feels natural and comfortable with them. His attitude toward sex is healthy, natural, and logical. He does not use his sexuality or his exterior as a tool to accomplish his objectives, but as a way of expressing his profound emotions and connecting to and uniting with the one he loves. The person experiences passion that is healthy for life, an energetic flow of creativity, enthusiasm, and happiness. He can cope with changes and accept them with understanding, and even with joy, because he is aware that they constitute a springboard to a new life adventure. He is full of curiosity about life, and feels that the changes are a continuous and marvelous adventure. He is the one who is in charge of his life and influences others through a feeling of unity and caring. When the chakra is balanced, the person can express and feel natural and true emotions toward other people. He is independent, but at the same time aware of the feelings of those close to him, and sees himself as a part of the community and society, and as an active partner. He derives a great deal of pleasure from life, on all levels – sensual and sexual pleasure, pleasure from food and drink, and intellectual and spiritual pleasure.

Unharmonious functioning
of the sexual chakra

Imbalance of the sexual chakra may derive from situations of imbalance in the age of development of the chakra, as well as from the period of sexual maturity. This period is fraught with feelings of insecurity concerning sexuality, with the search for oneself, and with attempts to define oneself as a member of a particular sex, and everything this involves. New sexual energies emerge in the person, and immediate society, parents and teachers are often incapable of providing the answers and teaching ways of channeling these energies. Often, these energies even cause damage via various unhealthy perceptions that cause the person to feel uncomfortable or ashamed of his feelings. This causes the adolescent to repress his feelings, to consider them unnatural and harmful, and damage his self-perception and esteem.

Of course, the situation is more serious when the person grows up in a particularly conservative environment, where sexuality is accompanied by a feeling of "prohibition" or of sin deserving of punishment. His attempt to repress his sexuality, which he keeps to himself, causes tremendous conflicts, as does the desire to subdue the sexual energy that the sexual chakra activates, and the feeling of enjoyment and pleasure from life. These situations can cause gradual and continuous damage to his abilities to express himself sexually, to his sensuality, and to his ability to make healthy contact with the opposite sex. The state of an unbalanced sexual chakra may be expressed in a lack of joy of life, being "tired" of life, a lack of creativity, a lack of desire, inhibitions and complexes.

Of course, the repressed desires don't just "evaporate." They simmer beneath the surface. The conflict between desire – be it sexual desire, or the desire for self-realization or creative fulfillment – and its non-expression or the inability to express it, may cause a feeling of constant dissatisfaction and emptiness. The person may try to fill this void with various addictions – to money, food, alcohol, casual emotionless sex, and so on. When this chakra is unbalanced, the person feels restless and unsatisfied, and has difficulty finding his unique path in life and realizing it.

It may happen that the person yearns for a satisfying relationship, whether emotional or sexual, but is unable to find the correct channel for his emotions and passions. He may live in this way, lonely and without satisfaction, for many years, without being aware that the root of the problem is actually within him. This can stem from continual repression of emotions during childhood or sexual maturation, repression of sexual desires, or from voluntarily foregoing – sometimes unconsciously – the experience of these desires on the physical plane. The messages that are transmitted to the world declare that "I am unable to express my desires." A great deal of balancing work must be done both on the sexual chakra and on the emotional and mental layers in order to liberate these unconscious suggestions from the subconscious, and permit new relationships to develop. This occurs through an energetic transmission to the universe of the desire for and ability to achieve these satisfying relations.

To the same extent, repressing desires that should not be repressed physically and emotionally may be expressed in the unhealthy realization of these desires, in rushed, hurried sex that lacks any deep emotional relationship (simply in order to "get rid of" the physical sexual desire), in excessive sexual fantasies, in watching too many erotic movies, and so on. Sometimes these expressions are accompanied by guilt feelings or an addiction to sex – real or fantasy. In any case, tensions and a certain lack of confidence toward the opposite sex are obvious. This lack of confidence may manifest itself in extreme "over-confidence" and Don Juan-like behavior, but its root nonetheless lies in a basic lack of confidence toward the opposite sex and toward sexuality in general.

The connection between the sexual chakra and the physical body

The sexual chakra is linked to the pelvis, kidneys, bladder, muscles, genitals, lymph, and all body fluids. For this reason, an imbalance in this chakra is liable to manifest itself in the deficient functioning of one of these organs and systems. This can be expressed in an imbalance in the body's circulation, in muscle problems, in kidney and gallbladder problems, and a broad spectrum of problems connected to human sexuality.

The kidneys, one of the principal organs for which the sexual chakra is responsible, represents shame, self-criticism and external criticism, disappointment, and a feeling of failure. Our personal yardsticks for success or failure, for "correct" and "incorrect," are in the main illusions that we ourselves have created. Our ability to accept the other, without criticism, judgment, or expectations, stems from our ability to behave in the same way toward ourselves – with self-acceptance. What is not acceptable to us is totally acceptable to someone else, and may even be part of the norms of another culture. Moreover, it is possible that in another incarnation, we ourselves perceived as natural and possible the very situation that we are condemning now in our present incarnation. For this reason, most of the borders, the limits, and the laws that we choose to believe in, may be illusions or excuses for a lack of self-esteem, reasons for self-condemnation. The sexual chakra is the source of joy, adventurousness, and the ability to see life as one long adventure that is packed with surprises – and so the errors, the mistakes, the disappointments, the guilt actually don't exist, because everything we experience is another adventure, lesson, or experience. When the sexual chakra is balanced and open, it does not mean that there will not be "disappointments" or "pangs of conscience." However, we can see things in the correct perspective, from the standpoint of self-knowledge and self-esteem. In this way, we know that even certain life experiences that we define as mistakes, as "incorrect", "negative", and so on, do not damage our self, because our self is not measured by "correct" or "incorrect", but rather simply exists in our particular way.

When the sexual chakra is not balanced, there may be a tendency for the person to measure himself according to his deeds, all the while criticizing himself and feeling that he has caused himself harm if he made a mistake. This leads to self-criticism, disappointment, and sometimes to shame, which are liable to continue for a long time, or become entrenched beneath the surface forever. In the same way that we perceive our experiences, we also perceive the actions of those around us, and criticize them or accept them as their own experience without defining it as "good" or "bad." Kidney stones and gallstones, too, often indicate profound and continuous self-condemnation.

The sexual chakra is responsible for the genitals, together with the base chakra which oversees the more physical layer of the organs. A substantial part of sexual problems that are not structural originate in clear mental causes. Our genitals represent our femininity or masculinity.

As we said previously, the sexual chakra is responsible for the way in which we perceive ourselves as men or women. What does it mean to be a man? What does it mean to be a woman? Those are the questions that are asked in the energetic center of the sexual chakra. Is there suffering involved? Or heavy responsibility? What are the contexts and the associations that we have regarding the sex into which we were born in this incarnation? How did members of the home into which we were born relate to sex? How do we think our surroundings relate to sex? Are we resigned to our sex? Do we feel that we are really "a perfect woman" or "a perfect man"? Do we accept and love our genitals in the same way as any other organ in our body? Do we accept our sexual feelings as natural? These questions have an essential effect on the state of our genitals.

The age of the chakra's development is in one of the stages when the young child discovers his sexuality. A lot of people experience traumas at this age when, completely naturally, they discover their genitals, examine them, and enjoy them, but are "rewarded" with a torrent of disapproval from their immediate surroundings. The beliefs that prevail in the home and in society pertaining to sex and sexuality affect the person consciously more during adolescence, when the sexual conflicts are likely to be clearer and more obvious. The belief that sex is bad, that the genitals are "dirty", "you're not allowed to touch them," and so on, can create a conscious or unconscious feeling of rejection toward them.

It is astounding to think that for thousands of years, the prevailing opinion in various cultures was that the genitals were "dirty and evil." This attitude led people to reject and despise a part of their bodies, a part of themselves! Many of the problems connected to sexuality, as well as the various sexual diseases, originate in this perception, which we may carry with us from our childhood and adolescence – and possibly from previous incarnations.

Today's perception of sex can be confusing. On the one hand, tremendous emphasis is placed on human sexuality, and we see so much sexual permissiveness in the media that whoever is not "sexual" enough is liable to consider himself imperfect and incapable of living up to the norm. On the other hand, the old, conservative norms still clearly exist in various social strata – so much so that the situation sometimes smacks of hypocrisy and duality. The need to be "good enough" in bed is one of the reasons for sexual problems such as impotence, premature ejaculation, and tension, fear, and pressure during intercourse.

Resentment and anger toward previous partners, out of a misunderstanding of the ways of the world – how we do or don't accept ourselves is reflected in our mate – are also likely to cause sexual problems. This is one of the reasons for vaginal infections, itches, and inflammations. Social beliefs, guilt, rejection of sexuality, the belief that sex and the sexual organs are dirty or "unworthy," tension, the desire to fulfill our partner's expectations from the sexual point of view (expectations that we ourselves contrive) and so on, all cause a large number of problems concerning human sexuality, the genitals, and the menstrual cycle.

In such cases, balancing the sexual chakra can be astonishingly strong, leading to far-reaching results, both in improving the deficient situation itself, and in adjusting the feminine or masculine self-perception and the perception of sex in general. Often, in order to treat the situation in the best way possible, it is necessary to bring up the traumas concerning our sexuality, directly or indirectly, examine them once again as another experience in this life, and free them lovingly. Balancing the chakra in conjunction with crystals, aromatic oils (that often help a specific problem), color projections, and Bach flowers, as well as meditations, guided imagery and other techniques, are likely to release sexual problems – even long-standing ones or ones that are considered to be "serious."

The influence of the chakra on hormonal activity

The sexual chakra is the chakra that affects the operation of the lymphatic system. This system helps cleanse the body of waste products. It helps transport protein to the capillaries and regenerate the volume of the blood plasma. It extends throughout the entire body, and consists of primary and secondary pipelines that become narrower until they are very thin pipes. There are various lymphatic centers that are responsible for different areas in the body. Lymph is part of the body's immune system. Bacteria and unwanted entities are trapped in the lymphatic centers, and the latter may swell up in certain cases of infection. This is one of the most important conveyor systems of the body. For this reason, when we ensure that the sexual chakra is well-balanced, we bring about a strengthening of the body, and increase its ability to fight external infections. The flow of the lymphatic system represents, as does the sexual chakra, our movement through life – the way we conduct ourselves in life.

The third chakra

The solar plexus chakra

Manipura

Location of the chakra: Below the diaphragm, from the sternum to above the navel.

Color: Yellow.

Complementary color: Purple.

Symbol: A circle surrounded by ten lotus petals, and inside it a triangle (generally red in color) containing the letters of the sound "ram." A kind of stem emerges from the triangle, describing the chakra's link to the central thread, to the spine, and to the rest of the chakras.

Key words: Assimilation, self-knowledge, logic, cause, doing, integration, personal strength.

Basic principles: Forming the personality.

Inner aspect: Desire.

Energy: Inner strength.

Age of development: From two to twelve.

Element: Fire.

Sense: Sight.

Sound: "Ram."

Body: The astral body.

Nerve plexus: The solar plexus.

Hormonal glands linked to the chakra: The pancreas and the adrenal.

Body organs linked to the chakra: The respiratory system and diaphragm, the digestive system, the stomach, the pancreas, the liver, the spleen, the gall bladder, the small intestine, the suprarenal glands, the lower back, and the sympathetic nervous system.

Problems and diseases that occur during an imbalance of the chakra: Mental and nervous exhaustion, seclusion, problems establishing contacts, gallstones, diabetes, problems in the digestive system, ulcers, allergies, heart problems.

Essential oils: Juniper, vetiver, lavender, bergamot, and rosemary.

Crystals and stones: Citrine, amber, tiger's eye, peridot, yellow tourmaline, yellow topaz, watermelon tourmaline.

Stars and astrological signs linked to the chakra: The solar plexus chakra is symbolized by the sun, the planets Mercury, Jupiter, and Mars, (Mars symbolizes activity and energy, assertiveness and power), and the signs of Leo, Sagittarius, and Virgo.

Virgo symbolizes analytical prowess, the ability to classify, acceptance of conventions, devotion, and service.

Leo, whose planet, the sun, symbolizes the splendor of the solar plexus chakra and affects it, symbolizes the qualities of the chakra that express strength, status, the need for recognition, warmth, power, and abundance.

Sagittarius symbolizes abundance, growth, and expansion, wisdom and experience.

The meaning of the Sanskrit name of the third chakra, Manipura, is "the diamond palace." The location of the chakra is the solar plexus, which is in the region of the diaphragm, and extends below the sternum to the navel.

The solar plexus chakra symbolizes our sun – the center of our personal strength. We absorb the life-giving and stimulating strength of the sun into this chakra, and as a result create an active link with the rest of humanity and with the physical world. The chakra is responsible for the development of our personality and the transmission of our emotions to the world. It directs our ability to influence our surroundings, our inner strength, and our intellect in its practical aspect. Via the solar plexus chakra, we connect to the world and interpret it according to the state of the chakra, and our emotions. It is the center of personal strength, desire, ego, and self-realization. Relationships with other people, the ability to enter long-term, balanced relationships, our desires, the things we love, and conversely the things that we do not love – most of these are directed by this chakra. This chakra directs our desire for recognition and for social standing, as well as for a clear identity in society, desire and aspiration for power, achievement, and for realization of our goals and aspirations, as well as for adopting social patterns.

This is the chakra that represents the ego. Part of our personality or ego is linked to building a rational attitude and to expressing a clear opinion about life, deriving from the ability to shape and form personal opinions. In order to have the ability to decide about life, ranging from the simplest things to the loftiest topics, we need to have an independent ability to form a personal opinion. Through the decisions we make in life, we are able to fulfill our potential completely. The process of defining personal power begins with the second chakra. It continues to the solar plexus chakra by creating a tighter link with the intellect and rationalism, which we use for forming an opinion and for making decisions concerning our world. The search for our individuality and self-definition, which begins with the sexual chakra, continues through the constant struggle with the reality of society's expectations of us, the social norms and conventions among which we search for our "personal line," which is not always in agreement with these conventions. We need the rationality, logic, and resoluteness of the solar plexus chakra in order to develop this personal line for ourselves.

The solar plexus chakra enables us to assimilate knowledge and experience. All the experiences, events, acquired knowledge, and empirical knowledge shape our personality and make us into what we are. Via this chakra, we grasp other people's frequencies and act accordingly. (In parallel, when we feel negative energies, the action of the third eye chakra cautions us against possible danger.)

The solar plexus chakra also has an extremely important role in our expressed spirituality. One of the chakra's most important functions is purifying the wishes and desires that are channeled from the lower chakras, consciously, by using the creative energy of those chakras for spiritual development, and for the transition to the higher chakras. From the spiritual point of view, the function of this chakra is to help us realize our vocation in the material world – to perform our life's function to the best of our ability by using our talents and capabilities, and to walk along our personal path of destiny in the material world to achieve self-realization in all the layers.

Via this chakra, the desires and passions of the lower chakras – the first and the second – are expressed and translated into a higher energetic mold that shapes our personality by connecting to the energy of the higher chakras.

Accepting and integrating feelings, desires, wishes, and expectations helps the third chakra become balanced and develop, because it increases the inner light and illuminates the situations and events that occur in our life.

When there is stagnation or blockage in the solar plexus chakra, the intuitive abilities do not flow smoothly to the higher chakras, and become concentrated in the lower layers of existence, by preoccupation with and focus on the material world. While this is happening, these abilities become limited. They will only become real spiritual abilities when they join and combine with the energies of the heart chakra and the third eye chakra.

When the third chakra is open, our ability to receive light

(and permit it to illuminate and glow within) is great and affects all of our functions. We feel happy, satisfied, and content. When the chakra is blocked or unbalanced, we may feel sad and even generally unbalanced. In addition, we transmit these states to our outer world, and make it gloomy and sad – or conversely, bright and filled with light and happiness.

Through inner wholeness and our ability to receive light, the third chakra gradually converts the yellow light of the solar plexus chakra, which expresses intellectual comprehension, into the golden light of wisdom, knowledge, and abundance.

Harmonious functioning of the solar plexus chakra

The harmonious functioning of the solar plexus chakra creates a feeling of tranquillity and inner harmony. When the solar plexus chakra is balanced, the person can contain his emotions and cope with his feelings, desires, and expectations of life. He considers his emotions to be an important and vital part of his development, and knows how to accept them in proportion. He does not react in an overly emotional way, but on the other hand does not curb his emotions. He is able to combine his emotions, wishes, experiences, and expectations of life into a whole. He feels at one with himself, with his role in life, and with his surroundings. He accepts himself while respecting the nature and emotions of others. The person's deeds are harmonious, exist in conjunction with the laws of the universe, and increase his abundance and satisfaction with life. But not only his. A person whose solar plexus chakra is properly balanced can feel an affinity for and unity with the rest of humanity. Their desires and feelings, just like the quality of life of those close to him, are important to him, and his actions and decisions include and take into consideration the good of those around him. The person feels energetic, active, assertive, independent, and tolerant.

When the solar plexus chakra is balanced, the person is enveloped in inner light that protects him from external negativity and from negative vibrations in his surroundings. The person feels sure of himself; he is courageous and creative, has a strong personality, and radiates inner strength and self-respect.

Unharmonious functioning of the solar plexus chakra

A state of imbalance in the solar plexus chakra is manifested in the person's fierce desire to control both his inner and his outer world. His ego is unbalanced, and his need for status and respect is extreme, to the point where he is liable to hurt others in order to attain respect and power. Manipulative behavior, abuse of power, arrogance, and extremely domineering behavior are likely to occur when the chakra is not balanced. The person feels the need to accumulate and hoard more and more power, and becomes excessively competitive and ambitious. Many of the people who are capable of trampling others underfoot on their way up the ladder of success suffer from an imbalance in this chakra.

When the chakra is in an unharmonious state, the person feels perpetual restlessness and dissatisfaction. This state may often be caused by a lack of acceptance during childhood and adolescence, leading to an inability to form honest and genuine self-esteem. The feeling of worthlessness induces a need for constant action in order to conceal it from the world, so that the person judges himself over and over again according to his success in the material world. He becomes horribly ambitious and needful of material achievements and success in order to feel worthy and to "prove" his worth to other people. This situation can make it difficult for the person to calm down; alternatively, it can get him into a state of inactivity and restlessness. The person is liable to feel that he requires constant action in order to feel worthy and adequate.

In these situations, status and material success may be the person's focal point to such an extent that he rejects the emotional world as being of very little importance to him. He may even tend to ignore or repress emotions that "get in the way" of this perpetual pursuit of success in the material world. He does not succeed in repressing them or attempting to make them go away, of course, and for this reason, all those repressed emotions are liable to burst out in various situations. The person is unable to control these outbursts, which may hurt him and, in many cases, other people. In many situations of an unbalanced solar plexus chakra, feelings of rage and bitterness toward parents and the world fester under the guise of a poker face, with the person pretending that "everything's fine" in order to appear successful and happy in the eyes of the world. However, the repressed feelings give him no peace, and he may suffer from bouts of depression or rage.

When the person perceives his inner strength and power as a means of control, a natural chasm separates him from the rest of humanity. He creates the "I – them" dichotomy. He classifies "them" into categories of "those who can help me accomplish my objectives" and "those who get in the way of accomplishing my objectives." He often establishes ties based on various interests, but is incapable of creating close and genuine social relationships. He feels as if he is one against many, against the world, and not a part of or partner in it.

His efforts to control and manipulate lead to a loss of a great deal of energy, and the person may find himself exhausted, needing external stimulants such as coffee, sweets, and so on, to the point that he needs them constantly.

Cases can arise in which the person is afraid of his inner strength. This fear leads to constant self-criticism, which is tiring and exhausting, and causes him to be cold and restrained (this derives from a basic lack of confidence and from self-criticism). In fact, the person is going against the chakra's natural energy, which is warm and full of enthusiasm.

The connection between the solar plexus chakra and the physical body

The solar plexus chakra affects and is responsible for the action of the diaphragm, the respiratory system, the stomach, the pancreas, the gallbladder, the small intestine, part of the large intestine, the adrenals, and the sympathetic nervous system.

The chakra's yellow color affects our sympathetic nervous system, and the emotions that are trapped in it affect the functioning of the respiratory and digestive systems. The solar plexus chakra is closely linked to the digestive process and the digestive system, and it is the main chakra that influences its action. The way we "digest" life, via the characteristics of our solar plexus chakra, has a significant influence on the digestive system. In the same way that we examine our world via this chakra, classify, absorb or emit the things that we encounter in our lives, so the digestive system is responsible for "classifying" foodstuffs. The liver is responsible for examining the food after it has been digested, for separating the valuable substances from the worthless ones, while the stomach digests the foodstuffs, and the intestine helps expel the waste products. This system operates in a manner that is parallel and similar to the absorption-storing-release of emotions. When there is an imbalance in the "digestion" of emotions, it is generally possible to identify situations of imbalance in the digestive system.

Allegorically, the liver symbolizes anger and the way we cope with it.

When the gallbladder functions deficiently, it may attest to stored grudges or jealousy. On the emotional level, gallstones can stem from feelings of pride, critical behavior toward others, and constant condemnation, external or internal, as well as from feelings of bitterness and "non-accepting" thoughts about others.

The pancreas symbolizes the sweetness of life. When the person feels that life is "bitter" for him, when he feels a desperate need for sweetness and affection, it is possible that pancreatic deficiency or even diabetes will occur.

The intestines represent our ability to release emotional waste, and to get rid of emotions that are no longer useful to us.

Many of the emotions of anger, helplessness, sadness, and loneliness, as well as various fears, originate in childhood. The mature person no longer needs these emotions. He is now a self-standing person who is no longer dependent on his parents or surroundings. Having said that, many people tend to hold on to these feelings, and do not release them. They allow this store of emotions to damage the way in which they perceive the world and their energetic transmission that shapes the reality of their lives. Intestinal problems frequently attest to the inability to release the old, the unnecessary emotional waste, and sometimes even the superfluous physical waste. This state may be combined with another state of imbalance that characterizes the disharmony of the solar plexus, which is stinginess and the inability to let go of material assets. In addition, when there is any kind of imbalance in the base chakra, the person also has existential fears and a need to hoard, and sometimes finds it difficult to get rid of things that he absolutely does not need.

The respiratory system represents our ability to inhale life – to operate in it, to flow with it, and to move in it. When the chakra is in a state of lack, the person is liable to allow life to flow past him without being involved in it by expressing his personal action and desires. In contrast, when the chakra is in a state of over-activity, the person is liable to "devour" life instead of inhaling it in a healthy and balanced manner. Both of these situations can manifest themselves in fast, shallow breathing, as well as in problems of the respiratory system.

When the solar plexus chakra is in a state of imbalance, this can be expressed in problems in the abovementioned organs, as well as in allergies and eye problems. Allergies, on the emotional level, can stem from an attitude of dislike or fear toward the world. They can also stem from the denial of personal power or inner strength, or oppression, as can happen in situations of imbalance of the chakra, and especially in cases of deficient functioning of the chakra, where it expends most of its energies on activities that are not in the least positive for the person. The eyes represent our world-view, the way we look at the world. Eye problems may indicate, in one way or another, our fear of looking at what is happening in front of us, or our hostility toward what we are looking at. Moreover, it may indicate a disproportionate view of various events in our lives.

The influence of the chakra on hormonal activity

The solar plexus chakra is linked to the activity of the adrenal (suprarenal) glands and to the pancreas. (See the chapter on the base chakra for a detailed description of the adrenal glands.) In the context of the solar plexus chakra, it is important to mention the activity of the suprarenal glands in the stress process. When we focus on the solar plexus chakra and begin to balance it, we learn to notice that our stress reactions are individual, and depend on the proportions that we attribute to various situations in our lives. Thus, they can be controlled and altered. When the solar plexus chakra is balanced, the person can avoid getting into repeated situations of stress. He is generally calm, self-confident, sure of his inner strength, and less susceptible to external and internal pressures. By balancing the chakra, it is possible to reduce and prevent stress as well as physical breakdowns and exhaustion that result from frequent stress.

The pancreas is an exocrine gland (a gland that secretes its product into the digestive tract or onto the surface of the skin and the mucus membranes) that secretes digestive juices into the duodenum. It is also an endocrine gland that secretes hormones into the bloodstream. The endocrine cells are located in structures that are called Islets of Langerhans. Those are clumps of cells inside the exocrine tissue of the pancreas. The pancreas secretes two main protein hormones whose action in regulating the glucose in the body and the feelings of repletion and hunger is absolutely vital. The first hormone is insulin, which is secreted as a result of a rise in the glucose level after a meal, causing the glucose to enter the cells. This in turn causes a decrease in the glucose level in the blood. In addition, it serves as a signal for the body's repletion, and causes the surplus foodstuffs to be stored, thus encouraging the free use of glucose for various purposes. In a state of hunger, a decrease in the body's glucose level causes a reduction in the secretion of insulin from the pancreas, and an increase in the secretion of other hormones that constitute a signal for hunger.

The second hormone, glycogen, is one of the important hormones that serve as a signal for hunger. The decrease in the insulin level, and the increase in the glycogen level cause the glucose level in the blood to remain constant, despite the continuous consumption of glucose by some of the body's tissues. A constant glucose level is essential for the body, since there are tissues (especially the brain) that must receive a steady supply of glucose. Because of the close link between the action of the solar plexus chakra and the pancreas, the balancing of this chakra is essential in cases of diabetes and problems in the insulin and glucose supply.

The fourth chakra

The heart chakra

Anahatra

Location of the chakra: Parallel to the heart, in the center of the body.

Colors: Green and pink.

Complementary color: Magenta.

Symbol: A circle surrounded by 12 lotus petals, and inside it a six-pointed star containing the letters of the sound "yam." The chakra's stem emerges from the six-pointed star. Another symbolic element attributed to this chakra is gray-green smoke.

Key words: Emotion, compassion, softness, love, balance.

Basic principles: Devotion.

Inner aspect: Love.

Energy: Harmony.

Age of development: 13 or 14 to 15 years.

Element: Air.

Sense: Touch.

Sound: "Yam."

Body: The feeling body.

Nerve plexus: The tactile nerves, such as the nerves in the fingertips that transmit the sensation of touch. (However, some people claim that the heart chakra is not connected to any nerve plexus.)

Hormonal glands linked to the chakra: The thymus gland.

Body organs linked to the chakra: The heart, the

circulatory system, the lungs, the immune system, the thymus gland, the upper back, the skin, and the hands.

Problems and diseases that occur during an imbalance of the chakra: Respiratory problems, cardiac pains, heart attacks, hypertension, tension, anger, a non-positive attitude toward life, insomnia, fatigue.

Essential oils: Sandalwood, rose, cedarwood.

Crystals and stones: Aventurine, chrysocolla, rose quartz, emerald, jade, chrysoprase, dioptase, malachite, rhodonite.

Stars and astrological signs linked to the chakra: The heart chakra is symbolized by the planets Venus, Saturn (since it symbolizes overcoming personal ego and striving toward unconditional love), and the sun, and by the signs Libra, Leo, and Sagittarius.

Libra, which is dominated by Venus, symbolizes the aspiration to balance and harmony, contact, love, and personal development.

Leo, which is dominated by the sun, symbolizes emotional warmth, generosity, and honesty.

Sagittarius, which is dominated by Jupiter, symbolizes abundance, growth, and expansion, wisdom and experience.

The meaning of the chakra's name in Sanskrit, Anahatra, is "the ever-beating drum." The chakra is located in the center of the chest, parallel to the heart, and it connects the three lower chakras to the three upper chakras. As a result, it constitutes the "heart" of the entire chakra system. It joins the physical and emotional centers to the centers of high mental activity, and to the spiritual centers.

The six-pointed star, which is located in the center of the chakra's symbol, symbolizes the link between upper and lower, and the meeting point between these two triangles – the upper chakras and the lower chakras – which is the heart chakra.

The heart chakra is the center for love, empathy, caring

about others, giving, devotion, and, consequently, the ability to heal. Thanks to its action, we are able to tune into the other, "feel" him, touch him, and let him touch us – emotionally, spiritually, and physically. The ability to connect to the other enables us to link up to the entire universe and to the divine force. Via this chakra, we feel the beauties of nature and the harmony inherent in it, and aspire to this harmony in all levels of our lives. Because of this aspiration to harmony, the chakra arouses in us the desire to feel the harmony that reigns in the different arts – music, painting, etc. – arts whose very existence stimulates and opens our hearts. This is the center in which words, sounds, and scenes are converted into feelings and emotion.

The heart chakra is located between the solar plexus chakra, which is the center for the basic emotions, and the throat chakra, which is the center for self-expression, and it is via the heart chakra that the basic emotions (from the solar plexus chakra) are purified in preparation to express personal power (in the throat chakra).

Thanks to the heart chakra, we can love and aspire to love. It directs our ability to give, to bestow, and to receive love, and it aspires to attain the ability to bestow unconditional, ego-free, and disinterested love, as well as openness to divine love. The aspiration to unity on all levels derives from it: from physical and tangible unity through love for one's mate to unity that stems from the love of nature and the universe. It also stimulates the ability to open up to celestial love and faith, which come from the fifth energy center, the throat chakra. Without opening the heart chakra, faith cannot be complete. The true aspiration is to unconditional love.

When the chakra is fully open and balanced, this kind of love, which is expressed for the sake of pure love only, cannot "get lost," nor is there any need or desire to "guard" it. When the chakra is not altogether open and balanced (which is very common), we experience fears of abandonment, fear of loss of love, and the misery of rejection. Unconditional love can never be rejected or forced.

When it is connected to the action of the upper chakras, this love becomes love of God and a feeling of the celestial power in every atom and component of creation. From this insight, the person sees the beauty and the divine in every person and creature, and can connect to the good and positive in it.

The heart chakra is also responsible for self-love, just as the solar plexus chakra is responsible for self-esteem. Without true self-love and acceptance, it is not possible to love the other entirely. The saying, "love thy neighbor as thyself" tells us that we have to love ourselves in order to be able to love our neighbor. When self-love is not complete, we discover our own flaws in every other person as a result of a lack of awareness.

The people who come into our lives frequently act as a mirror for our own personality, and when we do not accept our character traits, it is exactly those properties – directly, conversely, or indirectly – that will anger or bother us in others.

For this reason, on the way to acquiring the ability to connect to the force of the universe, our hearts have to learn how to love and accept ourselves and others.

From the heart chakra, we learn how to give of ourselves, forgive, excuse, and pity. Compassion is the ability to "feel the other," to empathize with his pain and sorrow with understanding and without judging him. The expression, "putting oneself into someone else's shoes" explains the essence of compassion. When we judge a person who is experiencing a problem, pain, or sorrow, true compassion cannot be realized inside us. Since we are not in his shoes, we do not know the burden of his present life or past lives. Man sees the exterior, while God looks inside us. The external appearance is often deceptive, and judgment prevents us from opening our hearts to love and empathy.

The basic emotions in the sexual chakra, which are activated in relation to the "I" in the solar plexus chakra, become conscious emotions in the heart chakra. In the solar plexus chakra, working on our emotions and acknowledging them leads to self-awareness and an increase in inner strength, while the wisdom that joins those aspects in the heart chakra opens them up to feeling the rest of humanity, and makes them less focused on the "I." When we open our hearts, we permit ourselves to be sensitive, and to expose our inner side and our softness. Softness is not only expressed in touch, but in the entire being. Steadfast self-knowledge and acknowledged inner strength are necessary in order for us to allow ourselves to be soft and emotionally exposed. However, this exposure enables us to be in constant touch with our own and other people's emotions, to receive love, and to remove the masks that we use to protect our soft inner side. When the solar plexus chakra is balanced, and the inner strength is aware and expresses itself properly, the heart chakra can permit the openness that leads to softness and acceptance. We feel strong enough to behave with softness and compassion toward the other, without the need to be constantly on the defensive, and wear protective "armor" in our relationships with those around us.

When the heart chakra is open and balanced, we feel inner faith. We understand that the power of God means love for every life form, and we are led to the higher function of the chakra, which is the ability to love not only those who are close to us, or human beings, but the entire universe.

The heart chakra is also responsible for another aspect of the deep empathy toward which it is directed in a balanced state: the ability to keep the "I" intact, and not identify with the other so much that the self is swallowed up, nor does it allow the pains of the other to filter into the "self." This aspect is important for everyone – especially for therapists. Even when we are prepared to help a person with our entire being – to give of ourselves with no intention of being rewarded and without any other self-interest, the same cut-off point is necessary for the integrity and health of the self. Over-identification can be a sign that the heart chakra is not properly balanced. When the person "drowns" in another person's troubles to the point that they disrupt his basic equilibrium, or affect his functioning, his reward turns into loss. In order to give, the person has to maintain a solid and connected center that is not swept away in the other person's torrent of pain and problems. There is a need for the ability to distance oneself in order to gain the objectivity that enables the person to see things in proportion, thus giving the other person the assistance he really needs. The ability to detach oneself and see things from the side, even if one feels genuine involvement and a sincere desire to help and to bestow love and compassion, also comes from the energetic activities of the heart chakra.

Harmonious functioning of the heart chakra

When the heart chakra is balanced, it has a beneficial influence on all the other chakras. The heart chakra links them together, since it is located between the upper three and the lower three chakras. When the chakra is balanced, it operates in harmony with the other chakras by helping the person become a channel that receives divine love and causes it to flow. The chakra's outward radiation onto the rest of humanity and the universe is tremendous. The activity of the properly-balanced heart chakra, especially when that balance exists in the other chakras as well, grants the person enormous power of love, which flows abundantly, consciously and unconsciously, over the people around him.

This state creates a person who is sought after and pleasant to be with, because his presence is soothing, consoling, and supportive. The person feels connected to other people, and empathetic and understanding toward them. He feels a powerful connection with those around him – but is nonetheless in tune with himself and emotionally stable. He himself feels happy and self-confident, and his presence inspires similar feelings in the people around him. In his company, they feel free, uncensured, and able to open their hearts easily. People whose heart chakra is open and balanced occasionally get reactions such as "You've helped me so much!" or "This talk with you has really helped me!" when in fact they hardly said anything – they just listened with understanding and affection! It is very easy to "spill one's guts" to such a person, and to feel that one has been given help and genuine relief, even if the person did not help actively or offer advice. Just being around a person whose heart chakra is open and balanced is truly "infectious." The energetic interaction causes the people around him "to open up their hearts," so that the person feels as if he himself has been given affection and understanding by people he knows as well as from strangers. This creates a pleasant and harmonious life in which the person encounters smiling faces and the desire to help wherever he goes (even from strangers in unfamiliar places), since the effect of an open and balanced heart chakra on the surroundings is enormous, and attracts love to its owner.

When the chakra is open and balanced, the person feels a desire to help, and an ability to be empathetic, and this is absolutely natural. Having said that, when the chakra is fully balanced, energy cannot be "sucked" from him, nor can he be exhausted or his good will exploited. He himself is aware of what he can give and knows his inner limits. The help he gives others does not serve to satisfy his ego or to make him feel superior to the person he is helping – rather, it is natural and flowing. A person whose heart chakra is open and balanced may offer assistance that is not exactly what the asker had in mind, but it is the *appropriate and correct* assistance, because the person can remain objective and discern what the other person really needs.

From the emotional point of view, an open and balanced heart chakra causes the person to accept his emotions totally naturally, without conflicts or a lack of confidence in them. He is not afraid of expressing his feelings, nor is he shocked by other people expressing theirs to him – by crying, cheerfulness, exuding warmth, and so on – since they are absolutely natural. Because he is able to accept his own feelings, he is blessed with the ability to accept and understand other people's. He considers the feelings legitimate and positive, and he will encourage the people to express them, not to repress them. The more balanced the rest of the chakras, with no inhibiting spiritual or psychological factors, the more pleasant it becomes to be in the company of the person with the open heart chakra. Of course, this affects his family and social relationships, and creates harmony wherever he goes.

As we said previously, the effect of an open and balanced heart chakra on the surroundings is tremendous. The fact that the chakra's energy flows freely creates an interaction with other people's heart chakras, and even people who are blocked and "hard-hearted" soften and reveal the love that is deep inside them on one level or another. The energies involved in the interaction with the soft and non-judgmental energies of love and compassion of the person with the open heart chakra can cause the hearts of hard people to melt and their anger to be assuaged and calmed. This is because their own heart chakra wants to be balanced (like the person whose heart chakra exudes warmth and love). In order to see how this situation works in practice, we can look at a familiar example: There is a car accident, and the two drivers pull up at the side and get out of their cars. One of them is red in the face, furious, fuming, and accusatory, even if the accident was his fault. The other, in contrast, is serene and relaxed, and forestalls the first one's yells by asking forgiveness sincerely, by apologizing in a respectful and empathetic manner, and by inquiring sincerely about the first one's physical wellbeing and the state of his car. It is often possible to see how the furious person, who occasionally uses attack as a form of defense so as to avoid blame, swallows his anger in surprise, calms down, and allows the person with the balanced heart chakra to involve him in a civilized conversation that is beneficial to both parties.

Self-love and acceptance, and love for other people, which become an inherent part of the life of the person with the open and balanced heart chakra, cause him to aspire to divine love – universal love. As a result, the person is aware of the laws of the universe, and operates naturally according to the cosmic dictum of "love thy neighbor as thyself". He understands that the sadness and suffering on earth originate in the separation from and inattention to the divine part of ourselves – to our soul. He aspires to connect, and understands that the initial separation was necessary in order to connect, just like death exists so that regeneration and vitality can occur. His will to live and his joy of life increase, and the world looks beautiful and welcoming. The person does not merely "live for himself," distanced from what is going on in the world around him, but rather feels at one with the rest of the creatures of the universe – human beings, members of the plant and animal kingdoms, the earth, and the celestial forces. His understanding of the laws of the universe enables him to view his personal experiences in a new light. Because of his correct emotional and mental interpretation of these events, he experiences certain situations – that may be traumatic or painful to other people – in a more understanding, profound, and tranquil way.

Unharmonious functioning of the heart chakra

Unharmonious functioning of the heart chakra is expressed in the various aspects of the person's ability to give and take. This state is liable to be manifested in a feeling that the person can give love, support, and help, but in fact he is not connected to the genuine nourishing and fulfilling source of love. Of course, this may cause mental exhaustion as a result of the person giving love when he is unable to accept love. He feels uncomfortable with displays of affection, and prefers to define himself as "a person who doesn't need others," since he interprets support, assistance, and accepting affection as weakness, and, in parallel, his giving can never be totally whole. This state is clearly expressed in various relationships, too. On the energetic level, however, it is likely to cause the person to feel unable to accept love, or feel unconsciously that he is not worthy of love. Accordingly, he does not attract or invite love to himself in the energetic layer. This situation is evident in all aspects of life. The more the person tries to convince himself consciously or unconsciously that he does not need love, the less love he will receive. This sometimes stems from experiences of rejection of love during adolescence, when parents tend to classify their child as too "big" for concrete, physical love. In this way, he learns to repress his need for love, and later on finds it difficult to accept love and displays of affection even from his mate.

Another situation that arises from the lack of balance between giving and receiving is the situation in which the person bestows, and lavishes warmth and love on his surroundings without being aware of the need to keep his center stable and balanced. He is emotionally blackmailed, in a state of constant giving, and feels that this is not reciprocated. We must remember that when the chakra is balanced, the person does not give in order to receive. He gives naturally and openly, and does not feel the need to get something in return, because the fact of giving is what is important to him. When the chakra is not balanced, the person feels a need deep in his heart to get something in return for what he has given. If he does not get anything, he feels disappointed and used and sometimes even bitter. When there is an imbalance in the heart chakra, the person's giving and affection may simply be a way of receiving affirmation, consent, or affection from other people. He fears rejection, and is afraid that if he stands up for himself, gives to himself, and concentrates on himself (when necessary), he will be defined as an "egoist" or will be rejected in some way. It is difficult for him to find the place in which self-love and love for others become one universal love, and feels that these two things are in perpetual conflict.

The connection between the heart chakra and the physical body

The heart chakra is responsible for the heart, the circulatory system, the lungs, the immune system, the thymus gland, the upper back, the skin, and the hands.

Despite the scientific claim that negates the supposition that we "feel" with our heart, the action of the heart is powerfully linked to the emotions we experience. Specific states of anger and irritation cause our blood pressure to rise, and when these states continue and recur, the condition can become permanent hypertension. When we experience loss, pain, or sorrow, the feeling of pain and emptiness often occurs in the chest, and when we experience relief from worry, we feel as if "a weight has been lifted from our heart." The heart is the organ that symbolizes the center of love and confidence: love for others and for oneself, confidence in oneself and in the universe. Ongoing emotional problems, worry that stems from a lack of confidence in the processes of the universe, and hurt resulting from love are experienced as severe traumas – all of them can be shown to be the emotional layer that is parallel to physical heart problems. Rigidity, hardness of the heart, a lack of caring, and ignoring the dictates of the heart in order to acquire money, power, and property are often shown to be the emotional layer that leads to a heart attack – or "cardiac infarction" in medical jargon. Hardening our heart toward our personal emotions and desires in order to receive society's affirmation of our existence can cause heart problems. The heart pumps the blood in our arteries and veins, and revives all the organs in our body. The life-giving blood represents the joy that flows in the body. When this joy disappears as a result of the heart chakra not being open to the beauty of the universe, problems in the circulatory system may occur.

The respiratory system, too, especially the lungs, is linked to the action of the heart chakra. Breathing is the expression of our ability to inhale life, experience it fully, and exist. When there is a lack of self-love, and the person is incapable of self-esteem and true self-love, this may manifest itself in problems of the respiratory system. The air we breathe – the element that is linked to the heart chakra – expresses the ability to connect to and be a part of the universe, on the one hand, and to define our personal space on the other. Conflicts between the ability to connect to the other and define our personal space at the same time are liable to be manifested in a range of respiratory problems. Asthma, one of the characteristics of an unbalanced heart chakra, is sometimes caused by smothering love, or by a feeling of choking that stems from the person's immediate surroundings. In children, it can be viewed as a kind of inability to breathe independently because of parents who "smother" them with love. It is not rare for the asthma to "disappear" when the child grows up and leaves home to go to college or to live an independent life. Having said that, the person can move out of his parents' home and still be deeply rooted in the same smothering patterns of love, without freeing himself of them. Consequently, he continues experiencing the distress of asthma.

The influence of the chakra on hormonal activity

The endocrine gland that is linked to the heart chakra is the thymus gland. This is a flat gland with two hemispheres that is located in the upper anterior part of the chest cavity, between the sternum and the pericardium (the membranous sac that encloses the heart). It is made of lymphatic tissue and plays an important role in the maturation of the immune system in children. It seems that T-lymphocytes, which are extremely important in the immune system, learn their function from the thymus. The thymus gland is the largest in size (in proportion to the body) in the newborn infant, and from adolescence it begins to decrease in size (in proportion to the body). In fact, it is in a state of degeneration in the adult.

The practical action of the thymus gland in adults is still a mystery. Despite huge progress in medical science, the exact action of the thymus gland in the adult human is still not known, but what is known is that its action up to adolescence is of crucial importance. It is a part of the lymphatic system, and up to the ages of 12 to 15, it secretes a hormone called the thymic humoral factor. It is possible that the gland is linked to the growth process, and to the person's progress from childhood to adulthood. Until the immune system is fully mature, the action of the thymus gland is absolutely essential. Even after that, it may still affect and stimulate the action of the immune system.

The fifth chakra
The throat chakra
Vishadha

Location of the chakra: The throat.
Colors: Blue, light blue, turquoise.
Complementary color: Red.
Symbol: A circle surrounded by 16 lotus petals, and inside it a circle, or a circle containing a triangle. The chakra's stem emerges from it.
Key words: Communication, expression, responsibility, universal truth, faith.
Basic principles: Nutrition, the resonance of existence.
Inner aspect: Communication and willpower.
Energy: Self-expression.
Age of development: Between 15 and 21.
Element: Ether – Akasa.
Sense: Hearing.
Sound: "Ham."
Body: The mental body.
Nerve plexus: The entire nervous system. (However, some people claim that the throat chakra is not connected to any nerve plexus.)
Hormonal glands linked to the chakra: The thyroid gland and the parathyroid glands.
Body organs linked to the chakra: The throat, the neck, the vocal cords and the vocal organs, the thyroid gland, the parathyroid glands, the jaw, the upper part of the lungs, the ears, the muscles, and the arms, and the nerves (not everyone thinks so).

Problems and diseases that occur during an imbalance of the chakra: Problems of expression, speech impediments, respiratory problems, headaches, pains in the neck, shoulders, and nape, throat problems and infections, vocal cord problems, communication problems, low self-image, a lack of creativity, emotional and thought blockages, ear infections, inflammations, and problems.

Essential oils: Lavender, patchouli.

Crystals and stones: Lapis lazuli, aquamarine, sodalite, turquoise, sapphire, blue lace agate, chrysocolla, blue tourmaline, blue quartz.

Stars and astrological signs linked to the chakra: The throat chakra is symbolized by the planets Venus, Mercury, Uranus, and Mars (which is the active planet that fulfills wishes), and the signs of Taurus, Gemini, and Aquarius.

Taurus, which is dominated by the planet Venus, symbolizes active self-expression.

Gemini is dominated by the planet Mercury, which is the planet of communication.

Aquarius, which is dominated by the planet Uranus, is the original sign of all the signs of the Zodiac.

The throat chakra's name in Sanskrit, "Vishadha," means "full of purity." It is located on the surface of the neck, in the region of the throat, with the petals on the front of the throat and the stem descending from the nape region. The throat chakra is the center for communication, inspiration, and human expression. The chakra communicates with all the aspects of communication – the self, other people, and the universal force (the communication manifests itself as faith). It joins thought and the expression of thought. This is the chakra that represents our self-image, and it creates an important link between the lower chakras and the crown chakra. It constitutes a bridge between our thoughts, our emotions, our impulses, and our reactions. Simultaneously, it transmits and expresses the contents of all the other chakras to the world. Via this chakra, we express what we are. In the previous chakras, the personality began to form, starting from the basic impulses and needs, via the unclassified basic emotions, self-definition, ego and aspirations, experiencing and classifying higher emotions – now reaching the ability to express this whole entity and present it to the world.

Via the throat chakra we express our vitality, laughter, tears, and our feelings of joy and love. This is the chakra that provides us with the ability to express consciously and clearly what operates and exists inside us.

The sexual chakra, which is linked uniquely to this chakra, is responsible for our creativity. The throat chakra supplies the inspiration. For this reason, it raises creativity to a level of artistic expression, and it is the chakra through which we release creativity into an artistic pattern – the written word (prose, poetry), music, the visual arts, dance, and so on. The passage through the chakras turns the creative energy of the sexual chakra into energy that is mixed with the desire for self-definition and expression, and then into the ability to feel and express emotion, and finally, into the ability to express creativity as an art that affects not just the creator himself, but also the spectators, listeners or readers of the work of art. This is an additional step toward the high and divine inspiration that is expressed in the third eye and crown chakras, which grant a dimension of wisdom, knowledge, and understanding of the universe to the work of art, as well as receiving divine inspiration.

The more developed the throat chakra is, the more the person can know and be aware of what is happening inside him. He is able to discern the impulses, needs, and emotions that are at work inside him, and from a certain distance, to clarify them for himself. As a result, he gains the ability to control and classify all of these inner activities, and he chooses which of them to project to the outside world, which to keep to himself, and which to release. Thus, the person has a capacity for free, objective thought, which is not affected by basic needs, or by irrelevant urges and emotions.

However, the significance of the throat chakra is not just expression, but also the ability to listen. When the person can open his ears – both the outer and the inner ears – he is able to receive profound knowledge from the universe. Listening creates tranquillity, calmness, and confidence, and together with the ability to discern objectively (that develops as a result of the chakra's action), the person can define his inner world, and discern what is happening in the external world in a clear and true way. When the inner voice is allowed to express itself, new knowledge about the "self" emerges.

The throat chakra is responsible for our self-imagination. If the solar plexus chakra expresses "what we are," this chakra expresses "what we think we are." When the chakra is open and balanced, the person is self-confident and has a positive and stable self-image that cannot be undermined. Whatever happens, he is still the same person, so he is not afraid of mistakes or failures, and they do not affect his fundamental self. The chakra's action induces a feeling of confidence and faith in higher guidance, and stimulates the person's desire to realize his cosmic vocation, which is beyond the realization of personal aspirations. From this, he aspires to self-expression that expresses all the layers of his being, which are higher than the physical and material expression.

It can be said that the throat chakra operates on two levels. On the lower level, it serves as one of the five lower chakras, and it can be linked to the basic element, senses and to the age of development. On the higher level, it is the first of the three upper chakras, and because of that it constitutes a link to the superego, to the soul, and to the spirit. When the three upper chakras are open, the person feels a true need to serve humanity. He feels that his vocation and mission in the world are linked in some way to bringing light to the world and to humanity. This feeling of vocation directs his life, in the same way in which another person is likely to lead his life according to a need to achieve obvious personal and material goals.

As a result of the chakra's dual-leveled activity, its activities can be interpreted according to both the lower layer and the upper layer.

The lower layer expresses the desire to attain satisfaction through expressing talents, desires, emotions, opinions, and so on. The person feels a need to use his voice and be heard, and to transmit his messages to those around him. On the upper level, the expression is linked to the person's spiritual qualities. It serves as an examination of self and of others, following a desire to ask new questions about the self, other people, and the world, in order to understand things in depth, and not accept them superficially and take them for granted. At this level of expression, the person is likely to use his expressive abilities – be they verbal, or the fruits of his personality or creativity – because of a desire to "give" something true, stimulating, and motivating to the rest of humanity. It is possible to see the difference between these two levels of expression very clearly in the different arts, especially the more popular arts. Today, there are many artists whose principal expression is that of their "I" and externalizing it. This action serves personal purposes – a need for recognition, self-expression, admiration from others, and so on. In contrast, there are artists who want to use their artistic ability to create a better world, increase the awareness of their audience, or provide the admirers of their works with mental and spiritual enjoyment.

The throat chakra is also the chakra that stimulates our sense of responsibility. This responsibility is expressed first and foremost in taking responsibility for oneself, for one's own development, and for one's personal life. On the higher level, this responsibility receives its meaning according to the concept of responsibility for others. This does not mean a need to interfere in or direct or control other people's lives, but rather understanding how my actions, my intentions, and my thoughts affect the world in general. On this level, the meaning of responsibility is reacting to the demands of the universe, to the superego, and to the higher goal. It expresses the ability to listen to and hear the call of the universe, which inspires the person to act for humanity and the universe, in accordance with his vocation and his path of destiny.

Communication, the essence of the throat chakra's action, can also be expressed in the lower and the higher layers. Communication is a vital need. It occurs unceasingly in the person's world – internally, as internal communication, and with the external world. The same essence of communication also occurs between our bodies, the physical body and the energetic bodies. The comprehension of this communication expresses one of the higher activities of the throat chakra.

As we said before, that same communication also occurs in the body itself, which reacts to external stimuli and internal processes. When the person is healthy, the inner physical communication and the communication between the physical body and the energetic bodies that contain the mass of emotions and thoughts, are taken for granted. In contrast, when some kind of disturbance occurs in communication – for example, when the person does not listen to his body, and pollutes it with unhealthy food or exhausts it in some way – the body reacts with unequivocal messages in order to draw the person's attention to the unbalanced state. Working with the throat chakra – opening and balancing it – leads to better and more profound communication with the physical body, and enables the person to listen to his body. To the same extent, it enables him to look objectively at the emotional and mental processes that he experiences (some of which can harm his physical, mental, and spiritual integrity), to relate to them accordingly, and fix whatever is in need of repair. This state generates a larger responsibility toward his body and soul. The person can view what is happening in his body and soul as something that falls within the realm of his personal responsibility, instead of getting involved with attributing physical and mental events to various external reasons. Examples of the latter are: "That guy annoyed me and made me angry," or "There's a flu epidemic now, and everyone's sick." He begins to look and to ask himself why these things occur, and where *his* personal responsibility and action lie in the framework of these events.

As we saw in the description of the link between the various chakras and the physical body, the source of every physical illness or disorder lies in a state of imbalance in one or more of the chakras, as well as in a particular thought or emotional pattern that permits the onset of the problem or the disease. When we can assume personal responsibility for our life and for our physical and mental state, as a result of the chakra's action, we can understand the way in which our patterns of thought and emotion create various physical manifestations in our world.

We can understand that we get angry when we choose to get angry and suffer from states of physical disharmony when we choose to cling to inhibiting and unhealthy thought and emotional patterns. Often, when the throat chakra is blocked or unbalanced in the extreme, the person finds it difficult to understand and internalize the way in which his thoughts and emotions affect his body, as well as the physical reality in which he lives. Sometimes this conjecture appears totally false to him, and he prefers to blame his hypertension on his "annoying and pressurizing boss," and has difficulty attributing his slipped disk to something that goes beyond "I made a wrong movement." In a certain way, this is resistance to assuming personal responsibility for one's life and a lack of faith in our ability to create our physical reality and affect it.

Communication permits awareness. It clearly proves to us the power of the word, and consequently helps us understand the power of thought. Via our communication – input and output – we transmit messages and receive information. We can understand the world and things that go on in it better, and clarify our opinions, ideas, and wishes. Today's sophisticated communication system makes it quite clear that closing our eyes to what's going on in the world is no longer possible. We know what's happening in almost every corner of the world, sometimes even in real time. The reaction time that is demanded of us today is also faster, and the messages that we send to the world arrive at their destination at a tremendous speed. Our perception of the world has to be broader. We can understand and internalize the fact that different people have a different mentality and a different lifestyle to ours. Peeking at their lives by reading newspapers or surfing the Net, by watching TV or listening to the radio, and discovering how similar they are to us, reinforces their humanity.

Communicative action is so powerful that it creates the future. When we react in a certain way by saying something, we create an instantaneous or continuous future. The utterance, "Pass me the salt," creates a possible future in which the salt will be passed to me. The utterance, "Come here," creates a possible future in which you are next to me. The way we navigate our external communication navigates the realization or non-realization of future reality, as well as how it will be realized. The same goes for both external and internal communication. The things we say among ourselves, the thoughts that are realized in our mental aura, have tremendous power to create our physical reality. The saying "think before you act," clarifies the realization of our thoughts in our environmental reality. Our thought patterns, both conscious and unconscious, direct the manner of our action and conduct on the one hand, and the way the universe reacts to us on the other, by realizing what we create in our thoughts. The stronger our awareness of the power of thought is, the more we discover that thought is a powerful tool for molding reality. When we are aware of this, we refrain from thinking destructive and non-positive thought (since this invites a similar reality), and adhere to constructive and positive thought so as to create that kind of reality.

Being aware of the power of thought, and understanding that thought is active and clear energetic power, leads us to the higher type of communication of the throat chakra. The higher communicative aspect of the throat chakra is the ability to become real in our thought as a creative and active force on the one hand, and to be attentive to the laws of the universe, to the superego, and to divine messages on the other. This higher ability links the activity of the throat chakra to that of the third eye and crown chakras, and when they are open and balanced, it is even possible to channel.

One of the additional key words that describes the action of the throat chakra is universal truth. In each one of us, there is an aspiration to truth that is expressed in the lower layers of the chakra's action as law and order. Law and order create a certain truth for us, according to which we measure certain activities, live according to certain norms, and create certain criteria. By nature, the person needs a certain feeling of justice and of conscience. Our personal feelings of justice, and of conscience, are greatly influenced by social norms, and when we and our surroundings operate according to them, we feel that "everything's OK."

However, these norms are mainly the results of human thought. On the chakra's higher plane of action, we are seeking universal truth. At this stage, the social norms that define truth, law, and order, may seem imperfect to us and sometimes erroneous or unsatisfactory. However, true wisdom enables us to discover and understand the laws of the universe, and to operate according to our inner truth, conscience, and integrity, by being directed to the pure laws of the universe, without creating a clash between them and the social laws and norms. From that, we can define for ourselves more clearly what justice is, for instance, while social justice, even according to its legal criteria, is not always clear and satisfactory. We may define for ourselves what truth is – is it action that is in line with what the person says, or beyond that, is in line with his inner thoughts and his general conduct? What is peace? Is it non-war, or is it the ability to accept the other in a whole and perfect manner, out of respect and esteem? And so on. Asking these questions creates our personal uniqueness, and inspires us to go back and discover the laws of the universe and universal truth that is found, awake or asleep, in each one of us.

Harmonious functioning of the throat chakra

When the throat chakra is open and balanced, the person can express his emotions, his thoughts, his opinions, and his inner knowledge clearly, fearlessly, and freely. When the chakra is balanced, the person feels sure of himself. Therefore, he is not afraid to expose his weaknesses or his inner power to other people. Self-confidence, a good self-image, inner integrity, and integrity toward others characterize an open and balanced throat chakra.

When the chakra is open, the person can control his speech. He can remain silent and listen attentively to what other people are saying, and he does not feel the need to raise his voice in order to make himself heard. The self-expression that stems from the opening of the chakra is manifested in all areas of life. The person feels able to express his personality, his opinions, his faith, and his creativity, in every field – in his studies, in society, at work, and with his family. He feels a certain stability, and no manipulations can cause him to deviate from his opinions, beliefs, and the paths in which he believes. On the other hand, he feels sufficiently stable to listen to and accept different opinions (that are acceptable to him); he is not afraid that this will harm his individuality in any way, nor does he feel a need to stand up for himself stubbornly without a logical reason. He can communicate in a clear manner in order to attain his goals. His manner of speaking is creative, and he has a well-developed imagination, but, having said that, he knows how to suit his words to his listener. The things he says are clear and bright. His inner integrity serves him well, even when he encounters various difficulties or temptations that are liable to make him deviate from his path. He is able to set limits, say "no" when necessary – but he can also be flexible in his opinions and look for ways to bridge and compromise between different opinions.

When the throat chakra is open, the person feels free, self-standing, and independent of others. He is decisive and self-aware, and can acknowledge both his weaknesses and his talents and qualities. Freedom from prejudice, and the ability to shape his personal opinions with a free hand are also properties of an open throat chakra. There is a unity between emotion, reason, and thought, and the person is able to operate according to his reason and thought without feeling torn between them and his emotions – both sides are equal.

On the higher level, the throat chakra creates the ability to recognize the power of thought, the ability to control thought, and also to subdue it easily when it is necessary to enter states that require a lack thought (such as meditation). The link with the superego becomes clearer, and there is an ability to recognize the various messages that are sent by the universe. The person can use symbols and understand them, create and feel inspiration and the power of imagination, and even channel with entities or thought energies on various extraterrestrial planes. The ability to listen, which characterizes the open throat chakra, attains a new dimension on the highest level. The person can listen "between the lines," be totally attentive to the people speaking to him, and discover in their utterances content that is beyond mere words. He can discern the qualities of the voice and the sounds that accompany the word, and give it a deeper significance. This ability is essential for therapists, because the patient often indicates the source of his problem "incidentally" or drops a hint during the conversation. Conversely, it is possible to understand a great deal about his problems and their causes from the way he speaks.

An open throat chakra allows the person to feel the joy of expression in all its forms. He is not afraid of saying what he has to say from the standpoint of his inner truth; he is not afraid that his opinions will not be accepted, or will be rejected by others, and is able to transmit, explain, and illustrate his opinions, conclusions, and beliefs to other people.

An open throat chakra stimulates deep confidence and faith in the person. Since it is the first of the upper chakras, it links us to cosmic knowledge and to the understanding that things are far from being what they seem on the surface, in their material and physical form. The self-expressive ability creates a feeling of freedom and the ability to understand the different functions of the people in the world, and to be tolerant of their opinions and their feelings. It creates inner depth, profound understanding of the ways of the world, and a feeling of fullness, satisfaction, and confidence in the universe and its ways.

Unharmonious functioning of the throat chakra

When the throat chakra is in a state of disharmony, the person finds it difficult to express himself, his personality, and his uniqueness on the different levels. He is fraught with various communication problems, and two of them are liable to cause severe conflicts and even a serious lack of harmony in all areas of his life:

The first is the communication problem between the person and his body, communication that can be blocked or unharmonious. The person has difficulty listening to his body and to its natural needs and desires. This state can wear him down, and he may be unaware of the nature of his personal functioning – this can easily cause him to succumb to various diseases.

The second communication problem is the inability to create harmony and unity between emotion on the one hand, and thought and logic on the other. This state can cause the person to be unable to express his emotions, or his emotions to be illogical or unacceptable to him, making him prefer to lock himself into a world of pure logic and intellect in which there is no room for emotion. This state can also occur when the person expresses unsolved emotions in his thoughts, but is unable to express them physically and verbally. He is liable to daydream and hold imaginary conversations with the people to whom he wants to express his emotions, but is unable to actually express them to the object of his feelings.

The imbalance in the throat chakra can also be expressed in low self-esteem, in a negative self-image, and in perpetual self-criticism. The person feels that it is necessary to behave, act, and speak in a way that "suits" others in order to be accepted by them. He is afraid of expressing his true opinions, which may generate criticism that will damage his already shaky self-esteem. Sometimes, an imbalance in the chakra may be accompanied by guilt feelings or a fear of self-expression and of expressing his personality. This can lead him to "cover up" his true opinions and desires with overtalkativeness in order to hide his true meaning, about which he feels groundless guilt.

The disturbances in communication that are caused by an unbalanced throat chakra can also be expressed in language and speech. The person is liable to speak haltingly, feel that he is not succeeding in expressing his thoughts in a clear and comprehensible verbal manner. Sometimes, the imbalance can be expressed in precise, to-the-point speech, which camouflages the fear of using too many words in case any of them should be "incongruous." People whose throat chakras are unbalanced are likely to always speak very loudly, or to stutter under certain circumstances.

The need that occurs, when the chakra is not balanced, not to "betray" the person's weak points, weaknesses, and helplessness is liable to cause him to always appear to be strong. He is unable to let himself be supported by others when necessary. This can exert a great deal of pressure on him.

An imbalance in the throat chakra can also be characterized in overtalkativeness, and talking for the sake of attracting attention. Gossip, too, which results from a fear of "awkward silences," and the constant search for a topic of conversation, can occur. The person may display problems in listening, or may hear only what he wants to hear, or understand what people are saying in a superficial way only.

When the throat chakra is blocked or unbalanced in the extreme, there is little likelihood that the person will become aware of and acquainted with the more subtle layers of the universe. A blocked throat chakra leads to a lack of self-awareness, which does not permit a broad awareness of the universe. This does not mean that the person lacks knowledge or understanding, but he is afraid of expressing this knowledge, or has difficulty doing so. It is likely that his awareness is expressed mainly in the thought and philosophical layer, but not in his life.

Because of the difficulty in expressing emotions when the chakra is not balanced, the person may become bitter or suffer from emotional outbursts when the repressed emotions refuse to be ignored any longer. Conversely, the imbalance in the chakra may lead to apathy and indifference as a result of the lack of good communicative abilities that help the person understand other people and feel an affinity for them.

The connection between the throat chakra and the physical body

The throat chakra is linked to the following organs and influences them: the throat, the neck, the vocal cords and vocal organs, the thyroid gland, the parathyroid glands, the jaw, the upper part of the lungs, the nerves, the ears, the muscles, and the arms. An imbalance in the throat chakra is expressed in a tendency toward numerous throat inflammations, infections and problems in the vocal organs, an imbalance in the thyroid gland (hypothyroidism or hyperthyroidism), lung problems, auditory problems, ear infections and problems, speech impediments and problems, stuttering, lung infections, tense muscles, neck pains, tension in the neck muscles, problems in the arms, and various nervous problems.

Fears of expression tend to become "trapped" in the throat muscles. This creates a blockage of emotions and thoughts, disrupts the natural energy flow, and creates limitations in natural expression. The throat is the organ through which we make our voice heard and express our thoughts, emotions, and desires. We express our creativity, our individuality, our personal opinions and our world-view through our throat. When there is a serious conflict between emotion and reason, or when there is repressed anger – a desire to express something, and a blockage of the desire – the expressive ability is harmed, and this can be manifested in throat problems. The throat is the center for our ability to change. It is located between the head and the heart, and for this reason must express flexibility and an ability to clarify our opinions and the way in which they fit into our personal lives. Rigidity and obstinacy, an unwillingness to change – even when the heart and mind indicate the need to do so – can also be at the root of various throat and neck problems. This is also the case when the person feels that he is unable to express his self and demand the fulfillment of his wishes. This is the function of the throat – to enable us to express what is in our heart, to speak for ourselves, and to present our opinions, desires, and thoughts. When a person stops himself from doing that, out of fear of his surroundings and of the way in which his demands or opinions will be received, he sabotages the original and basic action of this organ. This state is likely to be one of the causes of throat infections, especially recurrent ones. In such cases, it should be checked whether or not the person feels and understands his natural (and essential) right to speak for himself and express his desires, emotions, and opinions freely. Often, this is the source of chronic throat infections in children whose parents tend to speak for them, decide for them, or hush them up through criticism (in a direct verbal manner, or indirectly) when the child expresses his wishes or thoughts.

Losing one's voice is another problem that is linked to the action of the throat chakra. Like various throat problems, it may stem from continuously suppressed extreme rage and anger, to the point that vocal expression is prevented for fear that if the voice is released, the suppressed feelings of rage will also be. This condition sometimes stems from a deep, basic fear of making oneself heard, or from a trauma that caused this fear. Unfocussed thinking and an inability to concentrate can cause a person to lose his voice, because of a lack of knowledge of the direction in which he wishes to direct his voice in order for it to hit a particular target and express a certain wish.

Similar to the throat, the neck also symbolizes flexibility because of the fact that it enables us to look forward, backward, and sideways. When a person suffers from severe neck problems, tension, stiffness, and recurrent cramps that are not a result of prolonged physical over-exertion of the throat, it is necessary to check and see whether there are things "behind" him that he cannot look at, or if exaggerated obstinacy is inhibiting his development.

The emotional layer that represents jaw problems can also stem from an extreme repression of self-expression. The person feels that he has a lot to say – an emotional bottleneck and a large emotional burden that stems from unresolved conflicts between him and the figures who play a significant role in his life – but he grits his teeth and, with great difficulty, bottles up the emotional storm that threatens to erupt. Thought patterns that are full of vengeance, resentment, and rage can also cause various jaw problems, and are sometimes manifested in jaw-clenching during sleep.

Halitosis, when there is no obvious physiological reason for it (such as tooth decay or digestive problems) may well be connected to the functioning of the throat chakra in conjunction with an imbalance in the functioning of the heart chakra. This state may be an expression of unclean thoughts, venomous attitudes, and the habitual and frequent use of the mouth to expel mental "garbage" such as malicious gossip or hurtful, venomous words.

Problems in the mouth may also be connected to the state of the throat chakra. The mouth represents the way in which we receive nutrition – physically, emotionally, and spiritually – and the ability to absorb new ideas. Problems that are connected to the mouth may be the embodiment of narrow-mindedness, a lack of openness to new ideas, and stagnation of thought.

Stuttering is also a problem that can occur in cases of a significant imbalance in the throat chakra – occasionally in conjunction with a significant imbalance in the heart, sexual, or solar plexus chakras, or all of them. Stuttering may represent a deep lack of confidence generally, fear of expressing personal opinions, or the inability to express profound emotions. In the latter case, stuttering can occur when the person is trying to express his feelings about a particular person or matter.

The thyroid gland is the gland that is linked to the throat chakra. The hormones it produces are essential for maintaining the correct rate of metabolism in the body and for determining the body's rate of activity. Moreover, the hormones it produces increase the consumption of oxygen and the production of protein. Thyroid problems are often linked to a feeling of humiliation – the feeling of being "last in line" to fulfill wishes and desires, a constant need to take the desires and needs of others into account because of a low self-image and a feeling of worthlessness that causes the person to attract situations that "compel" him to forego his needs.

Hypothyroidism is a condition in which the thyroid gland is underactive, and metabolism – the symbol of our ability to receive and give in a balanced way in our life – becomes extremely slow (this occurs mainly in women). This condition represents resigning oneself to a lack of self-expression, not standing up for one's personal opinions, and not fulfilling one's natural desires and demands.

Hyperthyroidism, a condition in which the gland is overactive and causes an acceleration of metabolism, expresses a kind of "war" and inner resistance to this situation – resistance to the feeling of humiliation or oppression – a war that is waged without solving the basic reasons for being in the given situation. The person feels that he has to fight because of a feeling of no inner hope, in order to be "first in line," starting with his basic family unit and ending with his job, and in order to fulfill his desires here and now, as well as his capacity for self-expression.

Goiter, another thyroid disease, represents an extreme feeling of humiliation or the person's personal wishes being ignored by those around him – a feeling of exploitation. The person feels that he has to satisfy everyone else's wishes and do things for them, while no one wants to take his wishes into consideration and "do things for him." Of course, this situation expresses an unconscious perception of the laws of the exchange of energy between people – a state of constant weighing up "what he did for me, and what I did for him," which also causes a problem of unbalanced metabolism in the body. In the case of goiter, the feeling of oppression and exploitation is liable to turn almost into a physical mass of hatred toward the "exploiter" or the "oppressor." Moreover, goiter – which stems from the thyroid gland not receiving sufficient iodine, which it needs for its existence, and therefore creates a goiter whose job it is to absorb more and more iodine – can express a feeling of dissatisfaction with life. What there is in one's present life is not enough for a full and balanced existence. As we said before, the disease may manifest itself as a pattern of "rebellion" against the suppression of self-expression.

Deafness and auditory problems are also linked to an imbalance in the throat chakra. Deafness symbolizes a rejection of the desire to hear, and a desire to withdraw and close oneself off from the world. It is possible that, in the person's past, there were too many "painful" auditory stimuli, such as serious rows between his parents, family "secrets" that it was forbidden to reveal, verbal abuse, severe verbal humiliation, and so on. These things cause the feeling of "it would have been better if I hadn't heard." This may be manifested in different levels of hearing impairment, in accordance with the oppression and the messages or contents that were difficult to process emotionally, as well as with the person's level of sensitivity (or the child, as he was when these traumatic events occurred).

Sometimes, auditory problems express a feeling of excessive tiresome external stimuli, incessant parental verbiage that prevented the child from concentrating on himself, and "do's" and "don'ts" regarding everything, especially with children. Sometimes this is the reason for recurrent ear infections in small children, who are actually asking for a bit of peace and quiet.

The arms are also linked to the throat chakra. They represent our ability to hold onto various life experiences in order to learn a mental lesson from them (instead of perceiving this holding on as inhibiting or traumatic). A blocked and unaware mental ability to interpret life's experiences, feeling that life's difficult experiences are a burden, and a desire to throw in the towel and let things pass us by instead of grabbing hold of them and delving into them, can manifest themselves in various problems in the arms.

Many respiratory problems are linked to the action of the throat chakra in conjunction with a state of imbalance in the heart chakra. Breathing represents our ability to experience life fully.

Muscle stiffness may often be connected to rigid and inflexible thinking. Muscle degeneration is also linked, in certain layers, to the action of the throat chakra. It may derive from a loss of belief and faith in life, from a profound lack of confidence, from pessimistic, gloomy, and inhibiting thoughts that quench all desire to take an additional step in life, and from resistance to the joy of life that creates mobility. This state is also likely to stem from a tremendous need for "control," and also involves a profound imbalance in the solar plexus chakra.

The nerves, some of whose functions are linked to the action of the throat chakra, represent communication and the willingness to absorb. Nerve pains may derive from emotional pain whose source lies in deficient communication, or from guilt or punitive feelings that lead to an imbalance in the ability to communicate – emission and reception. The emotional parallel of a nervous breakdown may be the blockage of the communication channels, the breakdown of the desire to communicate with the outside world, or exaggerated preoccupation with the self.

In addition, there is a connection between sexual problems and the functioning of the throat chakra. Often, an imbalance in the sexual chakra parallels an imbalance in the throat chakra. Both chakras activate expression and creation, in different and complementary layers, so during treatment of sexual problems and problems concerning masculinity and femininity, the sexual chakra must be examined as well as the interaction between the two chakras. As we stated previously, the throat chakra is very important in our self-image, and some of the feminine or masculine sexual problems are linked to this layer of the person's soul.

The influence of the chakra on hormonal activity

The hormonal glands linked to the throat chakra are the thyroid and parathyroid glands.

The thyroid gland is located in the anterior part of the neck, and consists of two joined lobes. It is formed from the tongue in the fetus – part of the tongue becomes the thyroid gland. It is formed in the hollow of the mouth and moves downward until it locates itself in the neck. The gland contains follicles in which there is a substance that contains a large supply of the thyroid hormones triiodo-thyronine (T3) and thyroxine (T4). The thyroid is the only gland in the body that contains a large supply of these hormones. The amount stored in the gland is sufficient for the body's needs for three months. In order to produce the hormones, the gland requires two substances: Thyroid-stimulating hormone (TSH) or thyrotropin – a hormone that is secreted by the pituitary – and iodine – which the body absorbs from food, and is absorbed only by the thyroid gland because only this gland needs it. Inside the thyroid gland, the iodine synthesizes the two hormones, T3 and T4. The hormones are very important for the development of the brain and bones in babies. A lack of thyroid hormone in a newborn causes mental retardation and distortions in the development of the skeleton. In the adult, the hormone determines the body's "rate of action." On the cellular level, the hormone increases oxygen consumption and protein production. The role of these hormones in maintaining the correct rate of metabolism is absolutely vital.

The production of the hormone is regulated by the hypothalamus in the brain, which secretes a stimulating hormone called thyrotropin-releasing hormone (TRH). The latter causes the pituitary gland to secrete TSH, which causes the thyroid gland to secrete the thyroid hormones. A decrease in the amount of thyroid hormones in the blood causes a rise in the secretion of stimulating hormones, and vice versa.

The parathyroid glands are located on the thyroid itself, and dispatch the hormone that is responsible for the calcium level in the blood. The calcium levels in the blood plasma affect the activity of all the muscles in the body, including the heart muscle.

Thyroxine, a thyroid hormone, affects all aspects of the metabolism in the body, body temperature, and various growth factors. When the level of the hormone in the body is too high, as in cases of hyperthyroidism, the body has a tendency toward stress and over-activity that is likely to express itself in agitation, hair loss, increased appetite with weight loss, diarrhea, tremors in the hands, almost perpetual perspiration, an intolerance of heat, a fast heart rate, and exophthalmia (protruding eyes).

Too little of the hormone thyroxine causes all the body's activities including metabolism to be slower. In this situation, which is called hypothyroidism, there is a heavy feeling of fatigue, a lack of appetite with weight gain, hair loss, balding, swelling, slower speech, thickening of the voice, constipation, irregular menstrual cycle, sensitivity to cold, and major susceptibility to viral infections. (Note that every viral disease constitutes a mortal threat to the patient, because his immune system does not function properly.) This disease is more common among women.

Another disease of the thyroid gland is goiter. This disease occurs mainly when there is insufficient iodine in the food, or the ability to absorb iodine is impaired, and the thyroid gland grows in order to store more and more iodine.

The sixth chakra

The third eye chakra

Ajna

Location of the chakra: The center of the forehead.

Colors: Indigo, purple.

Symbol: A sky-blue circle surrounded on each side by two large lotus petals (or a lotus with 96 petals – each large lotus petal represents 48 petals), and inside it a picture of two feet. From the circle, the chakra's stem emerges.

Key words: Inspiration, spirituality, awareness, command, perfection.

Basic principles: Existential awareness.

Inner aspect: Extrasensory communication.

Energy: Intuition.

Element: Radium.

Sense: Intuition (the "sixth sense"), and all the senses in their most subtle significance.

Sound: "Ham-ksham."

Body: The high mental body.

Nerve plexus: The central nervous system.

Hormonal glands linked to the chakra: The pituitary gland and the pineal gland.

Body organs linked to the chakra: The brain and all its components, the central nervous system, the face, the eyes, the ears, the nose, the sinuses.

Problems and diseases that occur during an imbalance of the chakra: Eye diseases, ear diseases, respiratory tract problems, nose and sinus problems, facial nerve problems, headaches, nightmares.

Essential oils: Geranium, lavender, spearmint, rosemary.

Crystals and stones: Amethyst, azurite, fluorite, lapidolite, sugilite.

Stars and astrological signs linked to the chakra: The planets that are associated with the third eye chakra are Jupiter, Uranus, Mercury (because it symbolizes intellectual perception and logical thought), and Neptune, and the Zodiac signs are Sagittarius, Aquarius, and Pisces.

Sagittarius, which is dominated by the planet Jupiter, is linked to the chakra because of its comprehensive, holistic thinking ability, as well as its ability to understand inner processes.

Aquarius, which is dominated by the planet Uranus, is linked to the chakra because it symbolizes thinking that is full of inspiration from superior sources, superior knowledge, and developed intuition.

Pisces, which is dominated by the planet Neptune, symbolizes the chakra because of its developed intuition, richness of imagination, and the devotion that leads to higher truths.

The third eye chakra is located on the point between the eyes, slightly above the line of the eyes. Its stem descends along the length of the back of the head. The meaning of its name in Sanskrit, Ajna, is "command center."

The sixth chakra is responsible for conscious perception. It oversees the various mental abilities, memory, willpower, and knowledge. This is the chakra that connects the person to his subconscious, to his intuition, to the ability to understand cosmic insights, and receive non-verbal messages. It is responsible for the balance between the two cerebral hemispheres, the right and the left, that is, between intuition, emotion, and mysticism on the one hand, and reason and logic on the other. It is responsible for the person's physical balance, ability to concentrate, peace of mind, and wisdom.

The third eye chakra induces a desire for a feeling of wholeness, which stems from the perfect harmony of the universe. When the third eye chakra is blocked, people cannot imagine that this is possible. They live their lives by constantly struggling, compromising, resigning themselves – and see the existing reality as the only reality, which is obvious and cannot be changed by any force other than physical force and the force of practical action. When the chakra is opened, the person finds that he wants to feel in harmony with the universe, and first and foremost with himself.

The opening of the chakra arouses many questions. The desire for perfection is first expressed as a desire for self-perfection, self-integrity, and for faith in what the person does and in the feeling that he does not live for himself alone; there are higher powers at work in the universe. Man is part of these forces because of his soul. The awakening of the soul – or, more precisely, the awakening of the awareness of the soul – causes the person to query his vocation in life, and he often feels that so-called "ordinary" life – accumulating assets, financial security, work, status, and so on – is not enough. Sometimes this awakening creates a certain crisis, similar to the crisis that the person is likely to experience when his throat chakra is opened and balanced, when he realizes that in fact he does not express himself and his personality entirely. But this crisis is one of "recovery" – it leads to new insights, to openness that permits a deeper scrutiny of everything that is going on, and significant development of the awareness in all the layers. The quest for harmony that occurs when the third eye chakra is opened and balanced signifies a desire for the holistic harmony of body, mind, emotion, soul, and spirit.

The third eye chakra has a higher role in everything concerning creation – it is the one that links us to inspiration. The opening of the base chakra enables us to see to our basic and material needs in the physical layers of the universe, and to create our material world, which grants security and vitality. The opening of the sexual chakra enables us to express our creative powers as a result of self-discovery, adventurousness, curiosity, and understanding change. The opening of the solar plexus chakra enables us to recognize our inner strength and our personal power, and inspires in us the desire to create, while the heart and throat chakras require personal expression, and channels this personal expression into an array of artistic paths. Those same artistic paths into which the person wants to channel his physical, emotional, and spiritual energies all exist in the universe, in different forms. Movement, color, sound, structure, and all their derivatives, constitute part of the physical world, as well as the energetic and spiritual world.

The third eye chakra stimulates inspiration. As a result of inspiration, creation from nothing is possible – the creation of new worlds, inventiveness, the expression of higher insights and presenting them in forms that are somewhat comprehensible to other people, and the ability to receive messages from other worlds and other times – future or past – from distant places that the artist's eye did not see physically. The more open and balanced the third eye chakra is, the easier it is to enter a state of inspiration, which is known to many creators as a state that is timeless – like a meditative state in which an abundance of ideas take shape by themselves.

As we mentioned previously, the meaning of the Sanskrit name for the third eye chakra is "command center." On the physical level, this chakra is the command center for the action of the central nervous system. It oversees the regular activity of this system, which activates all of our perceptive and cerebral activities, and, of course, the senses. In addition, the opening and balancing of this chakra enables us to "take command" of our lives, possible only after we have understood the laws of the universe. As a result of the chakra being open, we can clearly see how we create our reality, and how we physically live the perception of our so-called "cerebral" world. Many people feel that they are in control of their lives, but in many cases, the opposite is true. The true "commanders" are the emotions or the thoughts that came into being during that life as a result of various life experiences and circumstances. When the chakra is open, the person can discern when his emotions – or non-supportive thoughts, as well as social norms, various acquired patterns, and so on – are in control. As a result of this ability to discern, he can sift out what is not "his" in the full meaning of the word – what does not belong to his soul fully and unequivocally. Equally, he can begin to discover what is "his": his true vocation, his true belief, the laws of the universe according to which the world operates (as does our life in its wake whether we like it or not). This ability to comprehend is tremendous, since it enables the person not only to realize his life according to his personal will, but also to realize it according to the will of the universe, which becomes his will.

As we stated before, the third eye chakra has supreme responsibility for the activity of our physical senses. On the spiritual level, this chakra is responsible for our intuitive ability, our extrasensory perceptive ability, and our ability to use our extrasensory senses. Just as the physical body has energetic parallels, so the physical senses have parallel, more subtle senses.

All knowledge exists in the universe. The ability to receive knowledge depends on the person's capacity, and on his ability to connect to those sources of knowledge via the third eye.

The vast knowledge that exists in the universe – in sight, sound, and sensation – is realized in sound, touch, and smell. We experience those senses through our physical senses.

However, each one of these senses exists in a more subtle form, in which the limits of time and space do not exist. The higher spiritual function of the third eye chakra is its ability to link up to these senses and activate them, and as a result receive vast, important knowledge, without being dependent on where we are, when we are living, or the physical condition of our physical senses.

The extrasensory visual ability (clairvoyance) is expressed in numerous ways. It can appear in dreams and meditations, and enables us to see things that are happening in other places, as well as at other times, including past lives or the future. Sometimes, this ability is activated when someone close to us needs us or is in danger. When the ability is more developed, the person can use it when he is awake as well by entering a meditative state, or with flashes of vision. Additional layers of this ability contain the ability to see various entities and auras, and look into the interior of objects or bodies.

The extrasensory auditory ability (clairaudience) permits us to pick up selected frequencies from among the infinity of sound frequencies that exist in the universe. It may be expressed in the ability to hear those who are near and dear to us, to whom we are connected with a direct, strong, and consciously based energetic link – or even the ability to hear divine sounds and messages from other worlds or from spiritual entities. When the physical auditory sense becomes increasingly refined, it leads to more "holistic" hearing – that is, hearing and absorbing more of the words that are spoken, and understanding the meaning of the frequencies of the speaker's voice.

Occasionally, this understanding is so acute that the listener is able to diagnose physical, emotional, and spiritual conditions according to the speaker's voice only. In addition, the clairaudient can pick up and hear what is not said physically, but rather only in thought, because what is said in thought is actually the energy of speech before it takes a concrete form.

Our ability to feel, the tactile sense, is a sense that can be highly developed. In its subtle layer, when the third eye chakra is performing its spiritual function, it permits the person to feel the different energies. This ability is used by many touch therapists. When we touch the recipient's body, we can discover the location of the physical blockages, muscle tension, warm and cold areas and so on through the tactile sense. When the tactile sense becomes increasingly refined, it enables us to touch the energy that flows from the various organs. Using this ability, it is possible to feel the subtle bodies and sense their condition, as well as the auric field of people and objects.

The sense of smell enables us to pick up different smells that occur as signs and symbols. The smell that is associated with the limbic system in the brain, the seat of the emotions, goes far beyond the action of smelling. We can smell something and suddenly feel overwhelmed by memories or emotions. This is because the sense of smell stimulates the limbic system, and "pulls" experiences that are associated with a certain smell out of it. In its subtle spiritual meaning, it enables us to smell things that do not exist physically. These smells sometimes occur as messages or symbols from worlds beyond.

The more open and balanced our third eye chakra is, the more openly and broadly our feelings can pick up events that do not occur in front of our physical eyes. The ability to pick up telepathic messages, in its different layers, is one of the expressions of the action of the third eye chakra. Telepathy enables us to "link up" to a certain frequency, to absorb it, and to process it consciously. The greater the awareness of the frequency, the clearer the nature of that sometimes vague "feeling" the person feels when another entity (human or other) tries to make contact with him. As the ability develops, it becomes possible to transmit an "answer" to the message that was picked up.

The ability to experience is not one of the senses, but rather includes all of the physical senses by adding the personal interpretative ability to what is happening. In the spiritual layer of this ability, it enables us to experience, consciously and through non-communication and separation of consciousness, experiences that we did not undergo personally or physically. Through this ability, all the abilities of the spiritual senses link up to create a perfect picture of events. This can be illustrated by the dream state. In certain dreams, the person feels as if he is undergoing the experience that is occurring. He sees a certain sight, hears the voices (or thoughts) that are spoken, sometimes feels tactile sensations, and is somewhat emotionally involved in what is happening. The spiritual ability of the experience enables us to experience another person's situation by holding an object that belongs to him, by observing or speaking to him, or through meditative states. It enables us to re-experience events from other lives, events from before we were born, and events that happened to us in the past. The last type of experience is familiar to almost everyone. We can re-experience, sometimes almost as intensely as in the original experience, a certain experience from the past, just by recalling it.

Thus it is obvious that the extrasensory experiences that are familiar to us – such as telepathy, astral journeys, psychokinesis (the influence of the power of thought on physical matter), prophecy, and prediction of the future, and so on – are affected by the condition of the third eye chakra. Of course, the cleaner a channel for receiving and transmitting messages the person is, the more clearly these abilities can be realized in him. While it is true that some of these abilities are "gifts" that are given to people on different levels, everyone can develop his spiritual senses to a certain extent, together with the ability to develop spiritual gifts they have been given.

Harmonious functioning of the third eye chakra

A state of balance of the third eye chakra, even if it is not completely open, is expressed in a good intellectual, cerebral, and philosophical ability, in an ability for research or invention, in clarity of thought, in high morality, in having good social roots, and in the ability to easily establish ties with people. One of the most obvious characteristics of the balance of the chakra is the intuitive ability, in all its manifestations. A balanced and open chakra (even partially) gives the person:

a good imaginative and visualization ability;
an ability to understand that is not only cerebral, logical, and rational, but also intuitive;
the ability to understand the embodiment of matter in the universe as a physical embodiment of the spiritual world;
idealistic thought;
free and creative imagination;
flexible thought;
the ability to see things from different angles;
the ability to discern how our thoughts, perceptions, and imagination exist and are realized in reality, through understanding the power of thought and imagination.

As the third eye chakra becomes increasingly open, endless perceptive experiences become available to the person. Things are interpreted entirely differently from those familiar "rational" perceptions, as a result of the ability to see beyond, above, and below what is happening.

The various intuitive abilities, together with the opening of the subtle senses, increase, and the person is able, according to his will (and not against his will) to receive intuitive messages that permit him to channel on different levels of awareness. The physical world is perceived as one world among the tremendous number of existing worlds. The insight that there are many different forms of life becomes clearer and more natural, to the point that in different layers of awareness, the person is given the opportunity to make contact with these forms of life and entities. The ability to feel, see, channel, and direct energies becomes clearer and more natural. The person can see the physical embodiment of his acts, emotions, and thoughts clearly, and as a result of deep insight, can match these layers to the action of the universe and to his cosmic vocation.

The ability to understand and even see previous lives increases, and the person is open to receiving messages from the universe, from his superego, from his soul and from his spirit. This can happen while he is sleeping, in dreams and meditations, and even when he is awake, as a result of understanding these messages, and the ability to use them in a useful way to repair his soul in this world and realize his cosmic vocation. Life experiences are perceived as lessons, as visions, as "learning aids," and as such, do not arouse inhibiting feelings, but rather the joy of learning and the ability to learn cosmic lessons that leads to the continuation of spiritual development.

As we said previously, there is no end to the tremendous abilities that take shape in the person when the third eye chakra is opened. When it is balanced and open, life becomes a marvelous experience, without a dull moment.

Unharmonious functioning
of the third eye chakra

When the third eye chakra is not balanced, the person is likely to experience his life via his intellect, rationality, and logic. He feels a need for order and logic in everything he does, and things that do not fulfill these criteria (such as some of the theories in this book) may seem absolutely impossible to him. He requires clear, logical proof of things. He has to see them with his own eyes or feel them with his own hands in order to digest, understand, and grasp them. In cases of a serious imbalance, emotion, too, and not just intuition, seems "illogical" to the person. Sometimes, this state can lead to an extremely limited, clear, and obvious perception of the world – everything that does not operate according to this perception simply does not make sense. Everything connected with spirituality is likely to be rejected out of hand as "not logical," or "unscientific." Despite the progress of science today, which provides step-by-step scientific proof of many of the spiritual theories, when the third eye chakra functions unharmoniously, even supplying scientific proof will not enable the person to understand these perceptions in depth.

Another condition of an unbalanced third eye chakra can – ironically – be manifested in the ability for basic understanding of spiritual truths, but only superficially. It may be accompanied by the desire to use powers of thought to influence events or people, to satisfy personal desires, to inspire awe or admiration, or to satisfy any other self-interest. This state generally goes hand in hand with an unbalanced solar plexus chakra, which causes the person to want to control and manipulate people and situations, and with the heart chakra, which is functioning in a serious state of lack or blockage. Among the people who suffer from this kind of imbalance in the third eye chakra are charlatans, who use their power to satisfy their selfish desires. The person whose third eye chakra is open properly never wants to use his intellectual or spiritual powers for any manipulation whatsoever. This is because a balanced state of the third eye chakra leads to a profound understanding of the laws of the universe, which do not tolerate this kind of manipulation under any circumstances. It also leads to a clear understanding of the danger, both personal and universal, that is inherent in the abuse of the power of thought or of the intuitive powers.

Sometimes, a situation may arise in which the third eye chakra is partially open, but is unbalanced, while the rest of the chakras, especially the lower ones, are not balanced. This can lead to a general imbalance, "floating," a lack of grounding, and an inability to understand the messages that are picked up by the intuition. A situation is also likely to arise in which the person cannot distinguish between genuine messages and visions that are the fruit of his imagination. He is liable to create various scenes in his imaginings, perceive them as genuine, and lose contact with reality.

A more widespread occurence is where the imbalance in the third eye chakra causes a lack of confidence in the universe and a lack of deep understanding of events. This lack of confidence may manifest itself in various anxieties, a lack of serenity, fear of the future, indecisiveness, agitation, constant tension, and cynicism.

The connection between the third eye chakra and the physical body

The third eye chakra is linked to the action of the central nervous system and to all the activities of the brain. It affects the face, the eyes, the ears, and the sinuses.

The eyes are the mirror of the soul. When the chakra is open and balanced, we can use our eyes to observe the person sitting opposite us and receive profound messages about him. The greater the spiritual awareness and openness to receiving non-verbal messages, the deeper the information (or more precisely, the feeling) that is received from looking into the person's eyes. We can see into his mind, and even into his soul.

The eyes represent the way in which we see the world. Our "world-view" (the way we view the world) can be affected by our present life – our childhood, our experiences, by self – and external teaching, by environmental norms, and so on. To the same extent, and often as a result of a direct link, it is also affected by our previous lives, because our soul chose those lives in order to explain previous world-views that were sometimes inhibiting or unresolved.

When spiritual awareness increases and develops, we learn to pay attention to the fact that our world-view, the way in which we choose to see things, is in fact our personal interpretation, seldom objective, and seldom "genuine" from the cosmic point of view. As a result of a subjective view, we attribute to the sights that are revealed to us different interpretations, which sometimes lead to criticism and judgment. We can observe the world benevolently or malevolently. The way we look at it is our internal choice and ultimately reflects the way in which we look at ourselves. Introspection is the foundation of spiritual development and self-awareness. Without introspection, it is not possible to understand the nature of external observation, which characterizes our relationship with others and with life itself.

The reality in which we live is directly influenced by the way we observe things, both external and internal. Since the human tendency is to give meaning to every sight, or seek some kind of explanation for it, we build self-insights. These insights crystallize into patterns. The resulting patterns are projected onto the universe – and whatever we project is realized in our world. For this reason, our world-view is what makes our lives real in this world. In the present, we can create our future by observation and interpretation alone. The more we know how to see things as they are – without the need for personal interpretation in order to "make order out of chaos"; without creating various patterns, some of which are inhibiting (and some supportive); without defining definitions – the more open we will be to accepting the world as it is. Accepting the world as it is immediately leads to accepting ourselves, and creates a situation in which the world accepts us as we are, without so-called external factors (since these factors are the ones that we invite, via our inner beliefs) disturbing the full expression of our personality and soul.

When the person observes the world malevolently, enviously (or is afraid to observe the world), or tends to see it in shades of black, or in black and white only, he may develop visual defects in his physical eyes. By looking into the person's eyes, it is easy to know how he observes the world – critically, fearfully, angrily, or with amazement, love, wonder, and curiosity. The more balanced and open the third eye chakra is (and the same goes for the other chakras), the more balanced and open the way of observing the world will be, thus leading the person to a happy, harmonious, love-filled life. The state of the third eye chakra also affects the ability to see beyond standard vision. It may be expressed in many different things, from seeing details in depth and an ability to observe profoundly via visions and hallucinations (in daydreams, meditation, or dreams), to seeing auras and energy channels, and infinite other aspects of extrasensory observation.

Our ears represent the way in which we listen to the world. When the action of the third eye chakra is involved, it is important to relate to listening not just as listening to sounds that are made or uttered, but rather to the messages that are received from the universe on the one hand, and to the messages that are received from the "I" on the other. Many cases of this hearing being blocked, as a result of all kinds of causes, can be expressed in various levels of hearing defects or various kinds of ear problems – frequently psychosomatic.

Our face is our "visiting card" to the world. When we look at a person's face, we can discover quite a lot about his temperament, because it is revealed on his face: laugh lines in the corners of the eyes, lips that are down-turned from worry or melancholy, a determined eyebrow structure, and so on. The expressions that are acceptable to us, that we tend to use perpetually, are radiated from inside outward to the face, and are imprinted in the memory of the skin cells, and this is how they create a certain kind of "visiting card." Our face signals to people to approach or to go away, it attracts or rejects, it is accepting and open or impenetrable. It can easily express our level of awareness. Since it is our "basket" of expressions, how we accept the world and ourselves is written all over it.

Facial problems can stem from various causes, and the problems themselves are varied, from acne to paralysis of the facial nerve. However, there is often a thread linking the different problems, indicating a need to present something to the world that is not in line with the inner "I," on one level or another. The saying "put on a happy face," actually means "show the world something that is not you at this moment" – in other words, put on a mask. The use of the face to exhibit something that is not the real "me" causes many problems in all layers – physical, mental, and spiritual. One of the first feelings that appears after the third eye chakra has been opened is that there is no danger or disgrace in being myself, and in presenting myself exactly as I am.

The third eye chakra is responsible for the brain and for the central nervous system. Our brain is our personal control room, the switchboard through which all the messages pass. But we are the ones that activate and direct our brain, and not the opposite. All our thought patterns are located in the brain, subject to our authority, whether we are aware of this or not. The brain contains a huge memory bank, a tremendous data bank, and information that can help us in every process. The more open and balanced the third eye chakra is, the more we can utilize the marvelous functions of the brain. We are the activators and programmers of a wonderful super-computer.

As we have written many times already (and repetition is necessary!), we are the ones who create our reality. The thought of today is the reality of tomorrow. At any given moment, we create and shape worlds by the power of thought alone. Recognizing this is a wonderful tool for development in all our layers. One of the things to which the work on opening and balancing the third eye chakra leads is recognizing this power, and understanding its unlimited uses. Because the chakra is the spiritual control center, it parallels the human brain in its function. The enormous potential its development offers are the same tremendous and infinite possibilities that make our brain unique.

When the chakra is not open (and may even be blocked), one of the first noticeable signs is narrow-mindedness. This is an expression of difficulty in accepting truths, experiences, and possibilities that apparently contradict fixed thought patterns that act as barriers against personal ability. The more our mental ability is open, liberated, and prepared to accept the world as it is, without limiting it to the "known" and the "familiar" according to various normative or emotion-dependent thought patterns, the more the ability to accept the best from the world and to be open to the infinite abundance of marvelous experiences increases and is fulfilled in reality.

An imbalance in the third eye chakra is often expressed in headaches, which represent an imbalance in the reception of messages, both internal and external. Sometimes, this expresses a lack of belief in oneself, fear, or self-criticism. When the chakra gets us to understand that we are all souls – clothed in the body and the life of this incarnation – and our lives here are but a dot on the infinite axis of time, self-criticism gradually disappears, and fear gives way to love and confidence in the universe.

Problems of an imbalance in the chakra can sometimes cause nightmares and various nervous problems. Problems in the pituitary gland, the gland that is linked to the third eye chakra, occasionally attest to a feeling of a lack of control of the thoughts, the body, the brain, or life itself. The ideal situation, which symbolizes the openness of the chakra, is the absence of the need for this "control" of life, through understanding that we are the masters of our lives, thoughts, and bodies. There is no need for a desire to control – control does not exist, in the long run – but command and direction do. When we understand that, the need to control disappears, and is replaced by a pleasant going with the flow of life that we create.

The influence of the chakra on hormonal activity

The third eye chakra is linked to the two glands that are located in the brain – the pineal and the pituitary. Very little is known about the pineal gland. It is located at the point of intersection between the (imaginary) horizontal line above the ears and the vertical line that goes up to the crown. It is a small gland, similar in shape to a pinecone. It is not yet known whether or not it is a part of the endocrine system. It releases a hormone-like substance called melatonin, which activates the cycles of the nesting, migratory, and reproductive instincts in animals. In human beings, the pineal gland is in charge of the internal diurnal and nocturnal clock, which affects our hormonal state and our mood. It is also responsible for many other functions. When there is any problem in this cyclicality, feelings of exhaustion, depression, and so on may occur.

The second gland that is linked to the third eye chakra is the pituitary gland. It is located in front of the pineal gland, and serves as a kind of command center that regulates many different functions. The pituitary gland weighs about half a gram, and it is located in a hollow in one of the bones on the floor of the skull. The gland consists of a body and a stem. The stem connects the body of the gland to the hypothalamus. The gland consists of two parts: an anterior part, which contains cells that produce the different hormones; and a posterior part, which serves as a reservoir and a place from where the hormones that are produced in the hypothalamus and transferred to the posterior part of the pituitary are released into the bloodstream. The pituitary is indirectly linked to the limbic system (the emotional center in the brain) through the secretion of hormones that are also linked to behavior and balanced emotions.

The hormones that are secreted by the pituitary gland oversee various activities, as well as the flow of additional hormones. The pituitary secretes two types of hormones:

Tropic hormones – hormones that are secreted from one endocrine gland and activate another endocrine gland.

Somatic hormones – hormones that are secreted from endocrine glands and directly influence the cells of the body.

The pituitary gland can be defined as a "factory" for the production of hormones, both tropic and somatic. Together, the hormones activate the body's endocrine system.

The hormones that are secreted by the pituitary gland involve all layers of physical and emotional existence. The posterior part of the pituitary secretes two hormones that are produced in the hypothalamus into the bloodstream: the first is ADH (antidiuretic hormone), which affects the kidneys and regulates the amount of water that is excreted in the urine. A small quantity of the hormone is secreted after a large amount of water has been drunk, so that the amount of water excreted in the urine increases, and the body gets rid of excess water. A large quantity of the hormone is secreted in states of dehydration, so that the amount of water excreted in the urine decreases in order to prevent the loss of water. It is of cardinal importance in the proper running of the body.

The other hormone is oxytocin, which is secreted in two cases: before and after birth. Before birth, it is secreted in large quantities and causes powerful contractions of the uterine muscles, as well as the opening of the cervix – in other words, labor pains. After birth, it is secreted in order to stimulate milk production during breastfeeding. (The role of the hormone in men is not known.)

The anterior part of the pituitary gland contains cells that produce various hormones. The secretion of all the hormones from this part is regulated by releasing hormones that are secreted from the hypothalamus.

The hormone TSH (thyroid-stimulating hormone) is a tropic hormone that regulates the secretion of the thyroid hormone in the thyroid gland, the importance of which was discussed in the chapter on the throat chakra.

The hormone ACTH (adrenocorticotropic hormone) is a tropic hormone that regulates the secretion of cortisol, a hormone that is secreted from the adrenal gland, which was discussed in detail in the chapter on the solar plexus chakra.

The hormone FSH (follicule-stimulating hormone) is a tropic hormone that is sent to the ovary and regulates egg development, the follicle-producing process, and stimulates secretion of estrogen in women. In men, FSH initiates sperm production in the testes.

The hormone LH (luteinizing hormone) is a tropic hormone whose function is to stimulate the production of the sex hormones in both men and women. In men, it regulates the secretion of the sex hormones from the testicles, and in women, it reaches the ovary and causes it to produce progesterone, to ovulate, and to maintain the pregnancy during the first three weeks.

The growth hormone (GH) is secreted all through life, but its level rises sharply toward the growth spurt (11-17 years), and it is essential for the growth of the bones in children. A lack of this hormone during the growth period causes dwarfism. An excess of the growth hormone, caused by the growth of the pituitary that secretes it during the growth spurt, causes gigantism (a very rare disease that leads to death at a relatively young age because of heart problems). It has been found that the pituitary secretes the hormone mainly at night, during sleep.

As we can see, there is no area of life that is not affected by the pituitary gland – just as there is no area of life that is not affected by the third eye chakra. If it is not open, spiritual life (and, in parallel, physical life which requires the hormonal command of the pituitary gland) will function defectively. To the same extent that the pituitary "commands" all the other hormonal glands, so the third eye chakra has the strongest influence on all the other chakras. When the third eye chakra is open, (even partially, and even if it is not fully balanced), and the rest of the chakras are in a state of imbalance or blockage, there is an overwhelming desire to balance the other chakras. Furthermore, they enable the person to recognize his chakras' state of imbalance, as well as the tools that exist to balance them.

The seventh chakra

The crown chakra

Sassharta

Location of the chakra: The crown of the skull.
Colors: Purple, white, gold, silver.
Symbol: A lotus with 1,000 petals.
Key words: Spirituality, insight.
Basic principles: Pure essence.
Inner aspect: Spirituality, infinity.
Energy: Thought.
Element: None.
Sound: "Om."
Body: The soul, the karmic, causal body.
Body organs linked to the chakra: The cerebrum.
Essential oils: Jasmine, frankincense.
Crystals and stones: Diamond, moldavite, clear quartz, selenite, smithsonite, pyrite.
Stars and astrological signs linked to the chakra: The planets that are associated with the crown chakra are Saturn and Neptune, and the Zodiac signs are Capricorn and Pisces.

Capricorn, which is affected by the force of the planet Saturn, symbolizes introspection, focus on the nature and essence of things, and the transcendence of the material.

Aquarius, which is dominated by the planet Uranus, is linked to the chakra because it symbolizes thinking that is full of inspiration from higher sources, superior knowledge, and developed intuition.

Pisces, which is dominated by the planet Neptune, symbolizes the liberation from limitations, devotion, unity, and recognition of the soul.

The crown chakra is located in the region of the top of the skull, with its petals pointing upward and its stem descending down the central energetic thread. It is also called the peak chakra. The meaning of the chakra's name in Sanskrit, Sassharta, is "the lotus flower with a thousand petals."

The crown chakra is the center of human perfection. It glows in all the colors of the rainbow, but its dominant colors are purple, white, and gold. It constitutes a limitless bank of knowledge, and the age of its development is infinite. It symbolizes enlightenment and connection to the higher layers of spiritual awareness.

The crown chakra unifies the energies of all the lower energy centers. It links the physical body to the cosmic energetic system and constitutes an electromagnetic center that provides energy to the lower centers. This is the starting point of the expression of all the energies of the rest of the chakras. This chakra is responsible for the link to supreme awareness, for the ability to receive divine and cosmic insights, and for the ability to connect to divine knowledge, to the light, and to universal love. This is the place where we feel "at home." There is no need to "do", no need to "control" reality, no need to think – simply "be" pure essence. This is the place that cries within us, "I am what I am," because of the clear knowledge that this life is just a manifestation of the soul in the body, at a certain time and place. It was chosen by the soul in advance in order to become familiar with reality in a certain way, by recognizing the points of light and "darkness" of existence (which in essence is all light).

Every emotion, every energy, every thought, moves along a vertical line, and the completion of that energy is on that line (that is, the line is an axis whose ends contain complementary "accumulations" of energy). On the same line, fear and love, sadness and joy, anger and self-acceptance, and so on, are located. We can choose to stand on one side of the line, which is fear, or on the other side of the line, which is love. In this way, through awareness only, we can easily turn darkness into light, fear into love, anger into self-acceptance, tension into understanding. From the crown chakra, we begin the journey to that life, which ostensibly constitutes a separation from the divine. From the crown chakra, we experience the unity with the divine that is us. Our personal energy field becomes one of the energies of the universe.

Everything in the universe is energy. For that reason, we can join, affect, and live in every single thing. Every imperfection that appears in front of our eyes is a reflection of the imperfection that we attribute to ourselves. This attributed lack of perfection may be the result of this or other incarnations. From the crown chakra, we learn to accept ourselves in our entirety – as an inseparable energetic part of the universe, as a soul that is experiencing existence in this dimension, as well as in other dimensions of existence.

In this chakra, everything we understand intellectually, cerebrally, and afterwards intuitively, becomes understanding and knowledge. Here, there is no such thing as the "why, what, how, where," but rather knowledge only. The knowledge that comes from the crown chakra far exceeds the knowledge that comes from the third eye chakra, because here we are no longer separated from the object of observation, but rather united with it. We do not see anything in the universe as separate from it. We understand and know that the other is in fact a part of us and a part of the universe, because we are energy that – only apparently – is embodied in a separate body. As a result, devotion, tranquillity, faith, and acceptance are awakened. We are no longer angry, nor do we reject or criticize what we see with the physical eye as being external to us. Rather, we know that that is part of us, that if we feel any objection, it means that we are objecting to what this part expresses inside us, to its reflection in us, as if in a mirror.

When the blockages in the crown chakra are opened and it receives energy fully and perfectly, all the remaining blockages in the other chakras seek to be opened. This is a result of raising our consciousness to a state in which we can, with thought and feeling, bring the nature of the blockage to the surface and liberate it through understanding. All the chakras vibrate at their very high frequencies, and each of the chakras acts as a mirror for the divine nature at its particular level, by expressing its full potential.

When the crown chakra is fully stimulated, we begin to radiate all the cosmic energies that we have absorbed, into the cosmos. From being the ones who are affected, we become the ones who affect the energies, the force in the universe that operates in unison with the universe, "workers" in the service of the divine light, which is us.

The crown center is opened during meditation, even if it is not altogether open on a daily basis. During meditation, the center receives divine knowledge that is later processed and understood via the other centers, and is expressed in thought, speech, and deed.

Harmonious functioning of the crown chakra

There are, in fact, no blockages in the crown chakra. It can be more open or less open, and more developed or less developed. With the opening of the chakra, the person experiences more and more moments in which the difference between external existence and internal existence becomes blurred, and disappears. He experiences many more moments of simply "being," in a state of acceptance – a state that does not involve needs, thoughts, fears, and so on.

Consciousness is completely calm, and the person experiences himself as a part of the pure essence that includes everything that exists. The more the crown chakra develops, the more frequent these moments become, until they become a constant feeling of balance and perfect harmony with the self and with the universe alike. The path to enlightenment, which becomes enlightenment itself, is likely to emerge suddenly as a kind of feeling of awakening to reality. The person feels that he is a channel for divine light and is prepared to receive this light at any time and in any form. Personal ego is no longer inhibiting, but rather constitutes a tool for carrying out God's wishes, and is instructed by the soul. There is no more resistance or conflict, but rather acceptance and reconciliation. The person translates the Creator's intention into deed, speech, and thought, and lets it take shape in the physical world. His personal path is the same path that he chose as a soul. The person understands and knows that now every question that arises is not another conflict. All he has to do is ask. He is able to receive the answers from the universe via his soul, which constitutes part of it. He does not feel the need "to do," but rather "is". He does not feel confusion or discomfort; but accepts himself totally, and knows how to see a meaningful sign in everything in the universe. He acknowledges emotions such as fear, anger, criticism, and sadness as additional tools for development and understanding, and knows how to withdraw into himself and examine them in depth in order to become familiar with their source and resolve them. Of course, he does not attribute anything to what is external to him. Statements such as "he annoyed me" or "she hurt me" and so on no longer exist, because the person understands that everything is one and every state of apparent imbalance is a reflection of what needs reconciliation and acceptance inside himself. As a result, he continues developing spiritually. He experiences life as a fascinating game. He understands that everything that happens to him is his own personal choice. It is clear to him that he is the one who chose this life, this body, and these experiences in order to become perfectly familiar with his soul through life in the material world. He understands that matter is just the realization in his awareness of the divine consciousness, and he does not actually exist as matter. When the chakra is open and balanced, the person gains enlightenment and a harmonious, satisfying life.

The characteristics of a crown chakra that is mainly closed

As we said before, there are in fact no blockages in the crown chakra, just states of being more or less open or more or less closed. When the crown chakra is not open satisfactorily, the person feels as if he is a separate, unlinked part of the universe and the essence. As a result, he is not free of fears and conflicts. His energies are not balanced, nor are they in equilibrium with the energies of the universe.

The person may feel that he lacks a vocation, that he is confused, not at one with himself, not fundamentally calm, and full of questions to which he does not know how to get answers. He is constantly bothered by the state of imbalance in the rest of his chakras. He may have a non-supportive perception of his existence, he may feel bored with life, or out of sync with people, situations, animals, and even objects. Fear of death, which stems from a lack of understanding of true existence, is liable to dominate or disrupt his life. He lacks a zest for life, self-confidence, confidence in the universe, and wholeness. He tends to shrug off responsibility for what happens around him, pinning it instead on other forces that he dubs "the others," "the world," and so on, instead of understanding that everything begins and ends with his personal choices. He feels that he has to "do," instead of simply "be" – thus realizing his personal action. He is likely to feel like a plaything in life's hands instead of being someone who has chosen this life. His capacity for spiritual development is small and his true potential is not realized. A very extreme result of a closed crown chakra may be expressed in extreme situations such as coma and death.

The frequencies of the chakra and the energetic bodies

The body that is linked to the crown chakra is the karmic/causal body. This body contains all the information concerning the previous lives of our soul, and its present condition. Linking up to and recognizing the karmic body helps us understand our vocation in this incarnation, the different patterns that stem from the experiences in previous lives, and the feeling of our soul in the present. It constitutes a kind of "forecast" of our soul. By linking up to the karmic body, we can understand what is going on in the present. We can understand why we chose this specific life, and what goal it serves in the perfection of our soul. We can discern if part of our soul is not here at this moment, and call it back and unite with it. Collective memories of humanity, from the past and from the future, also appear in the karmic body. For this reason, it can provide information about the past, present and future of humanity and the universe.

Reiki

Reiki is a Japanese term meaning "energetic spirit." It is composed of two words. The second word, Ki, is known in other cultures as Chi (China), Prana (India), Shakti (in Yoga), vitality (in the West) or Ru'ach Chayim (Judaism). In other words, this term is present in all cultures, and relates to the superior, all-encompassing cosmic energy from which all other minor energies in the universe draw their power.

Getting back to the first word, Rei is a general term for spirit or unseen spiritual quality, which serves as a channel or container for the Ki.

Many terms in different cultures speak of similar qualities. Whether called "Godly Spirit" or "Life Energy," the "Etheric Body" or "Cosmic Energy," the meaning is the same: There is an inexhaustible source of energy which may, if we know how to tap it, be conveyed through some sort of channel, revitalizing a living body (not necessarily the human body) and improving its quality of life both physically and spiritually.

In the West, the word Reiki is usually used, since the use of Reiki facilitates healing with this spiritual energy through a "channel". (The process itself is known as "channeling".)

Put simply, Reiki is an ancient known healing technique, in which healing is performed by the touch of a hand, in the same manner that a mother covers her child's injury with her hand, or a holy man or Shaman touches a sick person. However, Reiki affords us additional tools relating to touch, mainly allowing us to direct the flow of energy from a limitless source to the patient, in a meditative, spiritual manner, via the"tool" - in other words, the Reiki Master.

That is to say, Reiki teaches us how to be a channel for this limitless, ever-flowing energy, while enabling each individual to become an energy channel and draw the benefits of the Ki to himself and his patients.

The Five Principles of Reiki

Unfortunately, human beings cannot learn a new way of life unless they are first presented with the principles, philosophy and milestones of that new approach. By nature, these principles are worded concisely, in a manner which is easy on the memory, and constitute the basis of the entire doctrine.

The study of Reiki also includes these principles, known as the "Five Principles". However, since each Grand Master of Reiki, or great teacher, has devised his own principles, there is a difference between studying with one Master and studying with another. Some teachers propound four fundamental principles while others propound seven.

Setting the number of principles at five suits the Chinese way of thinking. They believe that the number five is the most basic of all numbers, the proof being the five elements (as opposed to the four elements of Western culture). Therefore, setting the number of principles at five is compatible with Chinese culture, one which has influenced the entire East.

1

The first principle of Reiki is the principle of anger, or, more precisely, non-anger. Anger, whether at oneself, at others or at the whole world, creates serious blockages in one's energy. This situation can be compared to a farmer whose fields are irrigated by water channels. Anger is like the large boulders which block the flow of water in the channels. Some fields are quickly flooded and their crops rot; others remain dry and their crops die of drought!

Anger is an individual's most complex inner enemy. Far from being fleeting, it becomes an integral part of one's personality. At the beginning, you may be angry at someone for one reason or another (and generally without any reason at all). Later you remember that you were angry at him and your anger is fired both by the thought that it was justified, and by guilt feelings that you were angry for nothing. And so, layer after layer of anger accumulates, and the nucleus of your anger turns into a great mountain of anger blocking the flow of energy and requiring a great effort for its removal.

Reiki, as a tool which directs cosmic energy to the place where it is required, is an excellent device for removing anger blockages which have accumulated in the body. However, the student reading this book should not be misled: All the Reiki treatments in the world will not overcome anger if the individual does not cease being angry. Reiki can remove anger blockages which have accumulated over the years (and, at times, even those which are a result of past lives). But Reiki cannot remove the residue of recurrent anger which occurs daily. This has been compared to a dog chasing its tail!

Do not be angry! This is the first principle of Reiki.

2

The second principle of Reiki is the principle of worry, or more precisely, the principle of not worrying. If a person's anger involves processes in which the individual relates to the past or present (we do not usually get angry at something that is yet to happen), the principle of worry deals with future events.

People, especially nowadays, have many reasons to worry about what the future holds. What will happen if I am fired from my job tomorrow? What will happen if I fall ill? What will happen if my favorite basketball team loses? What will happen to the rain forests in Brazil? What will be... ? Endless worries may fill one's head, and each one bores a small hole in one's body and soul.

Returning to the example above, anger is compared to boulders blocking the flow of energy, while worry is compared to large worms that bore through the walls of the water channels, causing them to crumble and leading to a leakage of water (energy) from the channel.

As opposed to anger, which requires a focused Reiki treatment in order to remove the obstacle, worry demands that Reiki energy spread throughout the entire body. Instead of removing the block, it seals and repairs thousands of small "holes". And as opposed to what a novice might think, it is much harder to treat problems relating to worry than those rooted in anger.

An individual who has experienced Reiki will quickly learn not to be angry, but it is much more difficult to teach such a person not to worry. Moreover, those who experience Reiki treatments are usually sensitive by nature, with hearts and souls that are open to the world and to society... And these are the exact foundations upon which worry is built.

In addition, it must be remembered that worry is not

always a negative phenomenon. Let us assume that you are a mother whose young son must cross the street every day on his way to school. Naturally, you are concerned about his welfare, so you warn him repeatedly about crossing only on the crosswalk, and worry daily until the moment when he enters the house safe and sound. Is it logical to suggest that you refrain from worrying? No. As a result of your concern for your child, you warn him to cross at a safe crosswalk, thereby helping him to protect himself. In other words, in this case, worry is a positive force, even though it is useful for one party (the child) while it drives the other party (the mother) out of her mind. What can a Reiki teacher do in this case? In addition to Reiki treatments, the teacher will have to find a middle ground in order to ease the mother's concern; for example, suggesting that the mother accompany her son to the crosswalk every day, or that she organize a voluntary crossing guard to man the crosswalk during those hours when children's safety is at stake.

Do not worry! This is the second principle of Reiki. Easy to say, but difficult to apply.

3

The third principle of Reiki is a positive principle – not one that instructs us not to be angry or not to worry, but one that may be expressed by the phrase, "Be grateful." A Reiki teacher that I once met claimed that if you smile at three different people throughout your day, you have fulfilled this principle. This is the essence of the principle – a smile, a good word, gratitude, thanks, forgiveness... simple things that might seem to be merely common courtesy, but which improve one's life and make one happier.

Remember that this principle is not only an external one. If you smile at everyone, always say "please" and "thank you", but do not mean it, you have not done anything at all for yourself (even if you have made others feel better).

The important element in this principle is inner intention, which is the only thing that benefits the individual.

My esteemed teacher defined it in the following way: " When a person is truly grateful, he radiates inner light and illuminates his surroundings. When a person is seemingly grateful but not does mean it, he is illuminated by an external light which originates outside of him but does not penetrate the aura enveloping him. Therefore, we might put it this way: Be grateful from your heart inward. This is the third principle of Reiki."

It is easy to apply this principle. It improves a person's life and the lives of those around him.

4

The fourth principle of Reiki is a general principle, simply stated: "Live a life of honor." This principle has many interpretations, although most teachers prefer to word it concisely and leave its interpretation to the individual himself.

The term honor means something different in every culture, and each Reiki teacher and student is fully aware of what the principle of honor means in his society. It should be remembered that honor exists amongst prisoners in jail, soldiers in the army, members of a family, teachers and pupils in schools, and so on.

Some teachers express this principle in a slightly different manner: "Earning a respectable living."

In other words, support yourself and your family respectably, without harming others.

5

The fifth principle of Reiki is that of honoring family, teachers and society, or, in other words, "Honor your parents, honor your teachers, honor your elders."

It seems to me that this rule should be obvious to everyone. Honoring the family protects family unity and creates a comfortable and positive environment for the individual and improves his daily life. Honoring teachers emphasizes the importance of knowledge and wisdom passed on from one generation to the next by the wise teachers of each generation. And one must remember to respect any person who has taught you something, whether he is an enlightened individual or just a simple teacher. Honoring our elders helps each of us remember that life is only a transitional stage between birth and death, and those close to the gates of death have already acquired much life experience and must therefore be respected.

Honor your parents, honor your teachers, honor your elders.

These, then, are the five principles of Reiki which every teacher and student must master: Do not be angry, do not worry, be grateful, live a life of honor, and honor your parents, teachers and elders. This is the entire Reiki philosophy.

Aura-Reiki

The principle of holding the hand

In the center of the palm, there is a point the size of a small coin. This point is located in the concave part of the palm, at a distance of approximately two finger-widths from the junction of the ring finger and the middle finger. In other words, when we activate Aura-Reiki energy, this energy flows from a little point in the center of the palm, and from there it passes and flows to the chacra.

The hand is held in two basic ways:

1. When the palm is held so that it is touching some part of the body, as if to join the opening of the pipe in its center to the opening of another pipe in the body – the hand is flat and adapts to the surface of the body part it is touching.

2. When the hand is cupped, and the Aura-Reiki energy is sent from the end of the pipe, traverses a short distance in the air, and penetrates the body of the practitioner or the recipient – the hand is a bit curved, as if to concentrate and focus the energy that is flowing out of the opening.

During Aura-Reiki treatment, the hands must face downward – as far as possible – with fingers close together, slightly cupped. That is, the hands are parallel to the ground as much as possible. This situation may change in various therapeutic positions or in self-administered Aura-Reiki.

When placing your hands on your own or the recipient's body, do not press hard, but just place them gently.

Aura-Reiki to the first chakra: The base (root) chakra

This placement is performed standing or lying on your back (not sitting). You can do it for up to seven minutes, exerting fairly strong, steady pressure.

The starting position for this placement is when you hold your arms straight at your sides, your hands facing your body. At the first stage, lift you arms and let your hands touch each other opposite your chest, your elbows touching your body. Let your thumbs touch the rest of your fingers (and leave them closed for the entire duration). Put your hands on your body in the area of the upper abdomen, fingers pointing downward, and slide them downward, gently rubbing until you reach the position of the pubic triangle shown in the picture. Your arms are straight or slightly bent at the elbows. Your thumbs (sometimes some of the fingers, too) touch each other.

At the end of the placement (which can take a long time), you must pull your hands to your upper abdomen, and from that point relax them and your arms by shaking them gently.

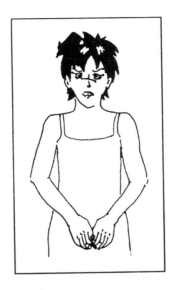

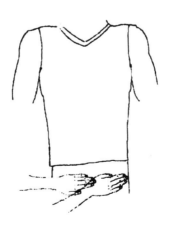

Aura-Reiki to the second chakra: The sexual chakra

This placement can be performed standing or lying down (not sitting, since sitting distorts the shape of the body and moves the hands out of the correct position). The starting position is when the arms are straight down at your sides, hands facing your body. First, bring your right hand to your body and place it, open-fingered, on your abdomen, with the tip of your thumb placed exactly on your navel and your pinkie on your pubic region. Add your left hand, with closed fingers, your left thumb touching your right pinkie. The pressure of the placement is gentle, and breathing is natural. When you perform this placement lying down, you can close your eyes. There is no time limit to this placement.

At the end of the placement, shake your arms and legs.

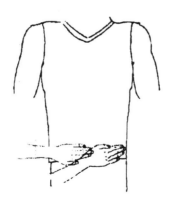

Aura-Reiki to the third chakra: The solar plexus chakra

The starting position is when the body is erect. Your hands are held in front of the chest, touching each other, elbows bent. The thumbs and fingers of one hand press against the thumb and fingers of the other hand. From this starting position, move your hands to the area of your upper abdomen (the diaphragm) with your elbows facing outward and your arms in a straight line, as far as possible. Your fingers are close together (on each hand) and your fingertips are touching. Your thumbs are separate from your fingers and parallel to them. Your fingers press gently on your upper abdomen. Your breathing must be deep, so that you feel your inhalation and exhalation in your hands. Do not close your eyes during this placement, which can be lengthy – up to seven minutes.

At the end of the placement, it is important to shake your arms and rub your hands together. You should walk around a bit in order to get your breathing back to its normal rate.

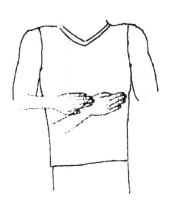

Aura-Reiki to the fourth chakra: The heart chakra

The starting position of the body is when your arms are held straight at your sides. First lift your left hand and place it on the location as in the picture. Lift your right hand and add it to the placement. Watch out for the placement of your right thumb – it must point upward. The placement is performed with the same medium pressure exerted by both hands.

This placement is an extremely powerful one, and has many uses.

At the end of the placement, shake your arms and rub your hands together.

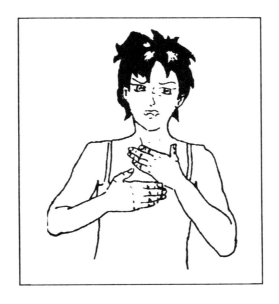

Aura-Reiki to the fifth chakra: The throat chakra

The placement can be performed for quite a long time. The pressure is weak. This is one of the only placements in which the arms (but not the hands) may touch each other.

This placement is performed sitting or standing, but never lying down!

Stretch your arms out in front of you at shoulder height. Your hands face downward. Bring your hands to your neck while bending your arms and placing your elbows as close to your chest as possible. Place your cupped hands (fingers close together) on your neck.

Take care not to press on your neck – this placement is meant to close a circle and not to choke you!

At the end of the placement, shake your hands and then rub your neck (as if washing it) with your hands.

Aura-Reiki to the sixth chakra: The third eye chakra

The placement begins with your arms straight and your palms facing your body. Lift your hands while bending your arms and place your right hand over your right eye and your left hand over your left eye. There is no contact between your hands, and the bridge of your nose serves as a "boundary" between your hands. Your nose and mouth remain uncovered. Your fingers and thumbs are closed, and your hand is slightly cupped (like a dome). Exert light pressure. Your head leans forward slightly in order to merge with your hands. Your eyes can be open or closed. (In general, if you keep your eyes open at the beginning of the exercise, they close during the course of it.)

This placement can be done for quite a long time – even up to 10 minutes.

At the end of the placement, remove your hands and blink your eyes a few times. Rub your hands together (as if washing them) and shake them lightly.

Aura-Reiki to the seventh chakra: The crown chakra

The starting position of the placement is with your hands turned upward opposite your chest. Your body is straight (sitting or standing). From this position, raise your arms upward and place your hands on your head, with your fingers together, as in the picture. Your hands are slightly cupped, so that there is a small gap between your hands and your head, but it is important that your fingertips press on your head (the root of your hands touches your head lightly). Your elbows face outward and slightly forward. The fingers of your two hands are touching, and the resulting shape is of an upward-facing triangle.

There are no time limits for this placement, and the only limit is that in this position, quite naturally, the head is pressed forward a little. In order to counteract this push, your shoulder-blades pull your back backward. When you feel tension in the body as a result of this pushing/pulling, it's time to stop the placement.

The placement serves as a personal expression of the link with the general Aura-Reiki energy – that is, when the practitioner submits a personal entreaty to the unlimited universal force.

At the end of the placement, lower your hands to your sides, and shake your body a bit to relax the tension.